143 SPECIES IN COLOR

TREES

A GUIDE TO FAMILIAR AMERICAN TREES

by
HERBERT S. ZIM, Ph.D., Sc.D.

and

ALEXANDER C. MARTIN, Ph.D.
Former Senior Biologist, U.S. Fish and Wildlife Service

ILLUSTRATED BY
DOROTHEA AND SY BARLOWE

 GOLDEN PRESS • NEW YORK
Western Publishing Company, Inc.
Racine, Wisconsin

FOREWORD

Trees brighten the countryside and soften the harsh lines of city streets. Each year they increase in importance and find new uses. They are beautiful and majestic; among them are the largest and oldest of living things.

Our thanks go to the many individuals and institutions who helped us with this book. Dorothea and Sy Barlowe, the artists, have given unstintingly of their time and talent to produce plates of unusual excellence. Leland Prater for the U.S. Forest Service has supplied invaluable photographs. Henry K. Svenson of the American Museum of Natural History, Harold N. Moldenke and the library and herbarium of the New York Botanical Garden, and William H. Durkin and Donald G. Huttleston of the Brooklyn Botanic Garden helped us over many rough spots, as did the National Herbarium in Washington, D. C.

In the present revision, nine pages of information have been added, including scientific names. We hope readers will find this fuller and more attractive volume more useful.

H. S. Z.
A. C. M.

USING
THIS BOOK

Trees are the most conspicuous and best-known plants in man's experience. Many are graceful and a joy to see. So it is no wonder that people want to know the different trees. This book is a guide to the most common trees in America. In addition to the 140 kinds pictured, the book may help you identify many more that are similar.

Trees are easiest to identify by their leaves. Most of the illustrations in this book show also the form of a tree as it usually grows. By studying the forms of trees, you may soon learn to identify them at a distance. This book deals only with trees. It does not include vines or shrubs. A tree is a woody plant with a single erect stem, growing to a height of 10 feet or more. While shrubs also are woody, they are usually smaller than trees and tend to have many stems growing in a clump.

This country has two major groups of trees: conifers (Pines and their relatives), identified by needle-like or scaly leaves; and the broad-leaved trees (leaves broad in contrast to leaves of the Pines). Some of the latter, like Willows, have narrow leaves. Others, like Maples, have broad ones. Trees with similar types of leaves have been placed together in this book to make identification easier.

One group of broad-leaved trees has simple leaves— leaves with a single, flattened blade on a stalk or petiole. Other trees have compound leaves, in which the blade is divided into a number of leaflets. A leaflet may look a good deal like a leaf, but leaflets are distinct in having no bud at their base.

The leaf blade may be entire; that is, with a smooth, uncut edge. The edge may be toothed, or it may have larger projections called lobes. Sometimes a leaf is both lobed and toothed. The pattern of the leaf edge permits further classification of trees—such as used here.

When you find a tree you do not know, first decide if it is a needle-leaf or a broad-leaf type. If the latter, see whether it is simple or compound, entire, or toothed or lobed. This you can tell at a glance. Then use the key (p. 5) to find where in this book the tree is likely to appear. Information in this book stresses identification.

Range maps show where various trees are likely to occur. If the range of more than one tree is given, a different color or line pattern is used for each. Overlapping of colors and lines means overlapping of ranges. Each species is named on, or next to, the color or line pattern it refers to, as in the sample map below.

As you learn more about trees, knowledge of their scientific names grows increasingly useful. Scientific names of trees illustrated in this book are on pp. 156-157.

Slip this book into your pocket or pocketbook. Use it in the park or along the street whenever you see a tree you do not know. Thumb through the book in your spare time. Become familiar with common trees, so you recognize them at sight. At first you will have to check details of leaf, bark, and perhaps buds and fruit to be sure of your

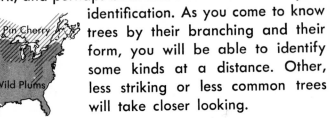

identification. As you come to know trees by their branching and their form, you will be able to identify some kinds at a distance. Other, less striking or less common trees will take closer looking.

A KEY TO THE TREES

Trees with needle-like or scaly leaves
(conifers) . . . . . **pages 18-40**

Trees with flat leaves of varying breadth
(broadleaf trees) **41-153**

Trees with simple leaves, not divided into
leaflets **41-129**

Edges of leaves neither toothed nor
lobed **41-53**

Edges of leaves toothed . . **54-81**

Edges usually lobed and toothed
(some entire); fruit an acorn **82-107**

Edges lobed, or toothed and lobed;
fruit not an acorn . . . **108-129**

Trees with compound leaves, divided into leaflets **130-153**

Leaflets arranged feather-
like **130-150**

Leaflets arranged finger-like **151-153**

SEEING TREES

WHEN TO LOOK   Trees are with us all year long and are as interesting in winter as in any other season. If you want to know the trees, study them month by month to see the changes that mark the seasons. Spring is a time of opening buds and flowers, some attractive, others small and easy to overlook. In spring, the pattern of opening leaves can be seen, with changing colors and textures as the leaves mature. In summer, leaf characteristics are obvious and should be used to the full. But the summertime leafy twig is not enough, for details of buds, twigs, and bark are easier to observe later. As fall comes in, many fruits mature and the development of rich autumn coloration, before the leaves drop, makes some trees brilliant. Winter is the time to study buds, twigs, and bark, and also to learn trees by their shape and form.

WHERE TO LOOK   Nearly every part of our country has its native trees and introduced species as well. Even the concrete canyons of great cities with their soot and fumes can boast of trees. Trees grow nearly everywhere. Florida leads the list with some 314 different species. Texas, Georgia, and California follow in order, but even the plains states boast of sufficient variety to make tree study worth while. To see the most kinds of trees in a region, visit as many different localities as you can.

HOW TO LOOK Look at trees in two different ways:
First, see them as a pilot looks at a plane flying toward
him or as you recognize your neighbor coming home from
work. A glance is sufficient; details are unimportant. You
recognize your neighbor so automatically that you might
find it hard to describe him. Learn to know common trees
the same way, so you can recognize a White Oak or a
Pitch Pine as you drive down the road. Learn the tree's
form and habit of growth so that you can quickly recognize it even at a distance, or at night.

Next, learn to look at trees as a student or scientist.
Notice details that identify an unusual species or tell you
about the growth and life histories of trees you know by
name. There is much to learn about familiar trees that can
be discovered only by close observation and detailed
study. First, you get acquainted with trees. Then, as you
begin to look closer, you begin to *know* the trees.

UNITED STATES FOREST BELTS

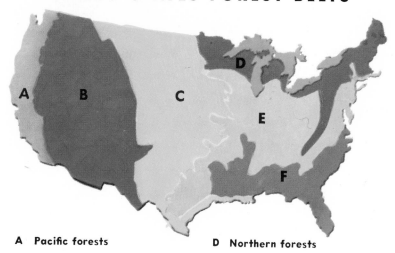

A Pacific forests

B Rocky Mountain forests

C Plains and prairie

D Northern forests

E Central hardwood forests

F Southern forests

WHAT TO SEE Trees are complex living things. Not only the leaves but the flowers, fruit, seeds, bark, buds, and wood are worth studying. The structure of the tubes and ducts that make up the stems varies from tree to tree. The annual rings in the wood show the tree's age and rate of growth.

Trees have flowers, though some hardly resemble familiar flowers of the garden. Detailed study of the tiny flowers can be as interesting as the study of large flowers such as those of the Magnolia and Tuliptree. The inconspicuous flowers of Oaks, Willows, and Pines are usually pollinated by wind. The larger flowers are often insect-pollinated. From the flowers develop fruits containing seeds; seeds too are worthy of study. Some are nutritious and have become foods for man and for wildlife. Some are dispersed by ingenious natural devices.

Study where trees grow. See them in relation to their environment. An unfavorable environment, as a mountain peak, may so dwarf and alter the size and form of a tree that one scarcely recognizes it as the same kind of tree that is growing tall and proud a few miles away. Some trees grow only in swamps; others only in sandy soils. Some prefer sun; some shade.

When you look at a tree, see it as a whole; see all its many parts; and finally, see the living tree as being in a community of plants and animals, living in close relationship to them and to the soil and climate.

KINDS OF TREES Trees belong to the same plant families as many herbs, flowers, and shrubs. Most of the 77 American families are represented by broad-leaved trees (p. 3). The needle-leaved species belong in the pine family with the exception of two yews. The palm and lily families include over a dozen unusual trees, and many minor families with only a few species are known.

MAJOR KINDS OF TREES

9

Over 800 species of native and naturalized trees grow wild in the United States. About 75 are naturalized; the rest are native. These trees make up over 600 million acres of forest and produce about 10 billion dollars' worth of forest products yearly.

PALMS: Over 15 kinds, with parallel-veined leaves, in warmer regions.

BROADLEAF TREES: Over 650 kinds, including oaks, maples, cherry, ash, birch.

CONIFERS: Over 100 kinds, including pine, hemlock, spruce, fir, cedar.

PARTS OF A TREE

LEAVES

Leaves make food from water and carbon dioxide, using the energy of sunlight. Chlorophyll makes this energy transformation possible.

Leaf of a Tuliptree

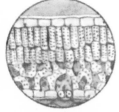 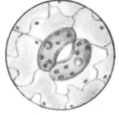

Inside a leaf, at the top, is a sheet of "palisade" cells which absorb sunlight. Guard cells around stomata (openings on the bottom of the leaf) help retain water.

Leaf cross-section and stoma (enlarged)

FLOWERS

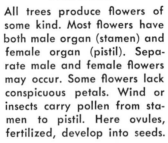

All trees produce flowers of some kind. Most flowers have both male organ (stamen) and female organ (pistil). Separate male and female flowers may occur. Some flowers lack conspicuous petals. Wind or insects carry pollen from stamen to pistil. Here ovules, fertilized, develop into seeds.

Tuliptree flower

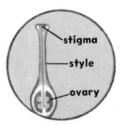

stigma
style
ovary

Pistil

TREE STEMS

The cambium is a layer of growing and dividing cells. Cells pushed outward form bark; those pushed in form wood, which enables a tree to grow large. Wood cells are long; their walls thicken and harden as they mature and die. Wood is mainly cellulose and lignin.

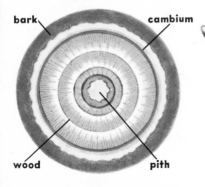

bark, cambium, wood, pith

Winter buds of Tuliptree

Wood and bark cells (enlarged)

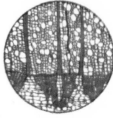

FRUITS

Fruits develop from the ripened ovary. They bear the seeds by which trees reproduce. Tree seeds vary greatly in size; some of the largest trees have the smallest seeds.

Tree fruits in various forms aid in the dispersal of seeds. Fleshy fruits are eaten by animals, from whose bodies the seeds may later be dropped. Winged fruits are spread by wind. "Seed trees" left after lumbering are a quick way to reforest land.

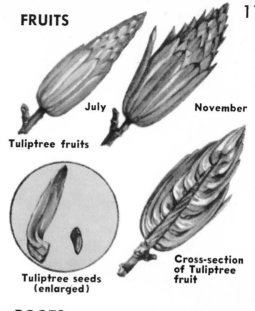

July   November

Tuliptree fruits

Tuliptree seeds (enlarged)

Cross-section of Tuliptree fruit

ROOTS

Roots anchor trees to the soil and absorb water and soil minerals needed for growth. Some trees have deep tap roots; others have a spreading system of roots.

Roots as they push through the soil are aided by a cap that forms over the tender growing point of each root. Behind this point, myriads of root hairs extend into the soil, increasing the root's absorbing surface tremendously. The spread of a tree's root system is at least equivalent to the spread of its crown.

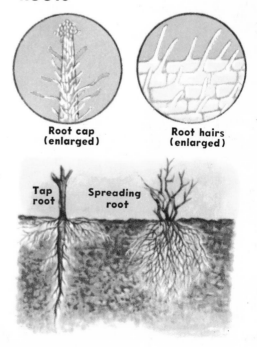

Root cap (enlarged)

Root hairs (enlarged)

Tap root   Spreading root

HOW WOOD FORMS

Twig cross-sections illustrated here show how wood cells grow:

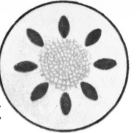

1. Tip of Shoot

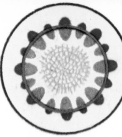

2. More Mature Twig

1 In a young shoot, bundles of cells form. These are a primary kind of wood, known as provascular tissue.

2 As the shoot grows, a layer of cambium forms across and between the primary bundles. As the cambium divides, wood and bark cells form.

3 The cambium layer continues to divide as long as the tree grows, forming wood and bark. Wood cells formed in fall are often smaller; growth stops in winter, and the spring cells are larger. This difference makes the annual rings in many stems.

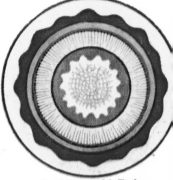

3. 3-year-old Twig

TREES AS LIVING THINGS are a wonder to behold. The oldest live for as long as three or four thousand years. Some grow almost as high as a 40-story skyscraper. The largest contain enough wood to build dozens of average-size houses. These giants grow from seeds so small that several hundred weigh not even an ounce.

Within each seed are the tiny beginnings of a tree. After the seed sprouts, years of growth follow, during which time the leaves use solar energy to make sugar from carbon dioxide and water. From sugar, by intricate chemistry, the wood of the tree is eventually built. The tree's center or heartwood is dead. But around this core is a living sheath from which all parts of the tree develop. As the cells of the tree live, grow, and reproduce, they use some of the sugar made by the leaves, minerals taken from the soil, and tremendous amounts of water.

TREES AND WOOD always go together. In very young trees and branches the growing cells develop a ring of vascular bundles. The very important cambium layer of cells forms across these bundles and soon grows to form a complete ring. As the cells of the cambium divide, those that are pushed outward form bark. Those that are pushed inward form wood.

Wood is made of several types of cells; most of them are long and tubular. Wood cells are alive when young; later they die, leaving a network of vertical tubes. Each kind of wood has distinct cells. Wood of conifers (softwoods) contains many thick cells called tracheids. Hardwoods contain wood fibers and vessels. New wood cells produced in spring are often larger and thinner than those formed later, and so each season is often marked by an annual ring.

WOOD STRUCTURE

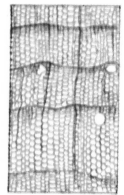

White Pine

Note the even-sized cells, the annual rings, and the few, scattered resin canals (which are more numerous in other pines).

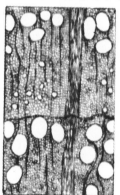

Red Oak

Oak is tough, hard, and often coarse. Note the large vessels which form in spring, making annual rings distinct.

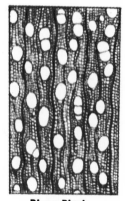

River Birch

In this even-grained wood, note the scattered vessels or pores. The annual rings are thin and harder to distinguish.

TREES AND MAN Trees always will be one of the important natural resources of our country. Their timber, other wood products, turpentine, and resins are of great value. Trees also have values beyond reckoning in holding the soil, preventing floods, and perhaps influencing climate. In addition, the beauty of trees, the majesty of forests, and the quiet of woodlands are everyone's to enjoy. The wooded parts of our country are the areas to which many people turn for recreation.

Woods and forests are the homes of many kinds of wildlife, ranging from deer, elk, moose, and bear to small squirrels and even smaller songbirds. Preservation of our timberlands and the conservation of forest resources are essential to a sound, farsighted national policy. Through the U.S. Forest Service, the National Park Service, the U.S. Fish and Wildlife Service, and many state agencies, forest and wildlife resources are being preserved or wisely harvested so that we may use them now, yet save them for our children's children to enjoy.

It is your privilege to have a share in the work of forest conservation. Do your share by being careful with fire, by helping in tree planting, and by being vigilant in protecting, through legislation, your forest and wildlife resources.

FIELD STUDY Trees can be studied at every season, and they should be. Study the life history of a tree through the year. Each season will show features that cannot be seen at other times. Select some nearby trees to visit at least once a month. Watch the buds open in spring and the leaves unfold. See the flowers, fruit, autumn color, twigs, bark, and even the insect pests. On page 154 are suggestions of excellent places to see and study trees. Specimens are often labeled to aid identification.

COLLECTIONS are not so important in studying trees as you might believe. Field studies are best, but a collection of leaves, twigs, or fruits may be of real value if you use the collection after you make it. Leaves are easiest to collect. Make your collection early in the season before insects and storms have injured the leaves. Get a short twig with several leaves, to show leaf placement as well as twig and bud characteristics. Press leaves between sheets of newsprint or other soft paper. Set a board atop your press with a heavy weight on it. Turn and change the papers daily or every few days.

After leaves are pressed, mount them on cardboard with strips of gummed paper. Turn some over to show

the reverse side. Cover with Cellophane. Label your specimen with common and scientific name, date collected, locality, and notes. Collections of winter twigs can be mounted on cardboard with thin wire. Seeds and fruits can be stored in small boxes or in glass vials.

TREE CENSUS   A census of trees can be interesting and valuable to both the census taker and to the community. Often the best argument for conserving or improving the tree plantings in your town or in nearby forests is a report on the existing conditions. Get a map of your town, neighborhood, or camp. Follow it systematically, marking down the location and name of each tree you find. Keep a count by species as you go.

GROWING TREES   Seeds of many common trees are easy to grow and cultivate as seedlings. A visit to a state or Forest Service nursery will show you how this is done. Collect seeds of common species. Most will not grow till the following spring and should be stored at outdoor temperatures. In spring, seeds may be set in flats or pots covered lightly with a mixture of sand and loam. Learn to recognize the seedlings, for they often have leaves that differ from those of mature trees. When seedlings are several inches high, they can be set in individual pots or transplanted.

FORESTS AND FOREST TYPES   Trees do not grow in an entirely haphazard pattern. Differences in soil, temperature, and rainfall tend to cause certain species to grow together, forming distinct types of forests, such as the northern coniferous forests of Maine or the Oak-Hickory hardwood forests of Ohio. If you travel at all, knowing and recognizing the forest types will add to your enjoyment of the scenery.

Pressed and mounted specimens.

FAMOUS TREES Most cities or regions have trees famous for their age, size, or historic events that took place nearby. Locate historic trees in your community; see that they get any needed attention. Search for the largest trees in your area; you may find record specimens.

REFORESTATION Careless lumbering, fires, hastily planned agricultural programs, and plain neglect have left our forest remnants in poor shape in many places. Often where this has occurred, local groups are taking active steps to restock the land with crops of trees. Schools can sometimes obtain farms abandoned for taxes, to be used for practical conservation demonstration plots. Other school systems have their own farms and camps to teach and practice conservation.

COMMUNITY FORESTS AND FOREST RESERVES There are, in this country, several communities free of taxes because the income from community forests, planted decades ago, is enough to meet the bills. A community forest is a project which does more than provide future income from lumber. It also becomes a wildlife refuge and, if the surroundings permit, a picnic and recreation center. Areas around reservoirs, for example, where use of the land is limited, are excellent for this purpose. Interest other people, then consult the county agent, state forester, or a representative of the U.S. Forest Service to make suitable plans.

WOOD AND LUMBER The recognition of different woods by their pores, rays, and grain is an interesting hobby, especially if you like wood and use it. If you collect and study woods, remember that the names that lumbermen give trees are often different from those used in this book. White Oak lumber may come from six or eight different Oaks; Yellow Pine from several Pines.

THE PINES

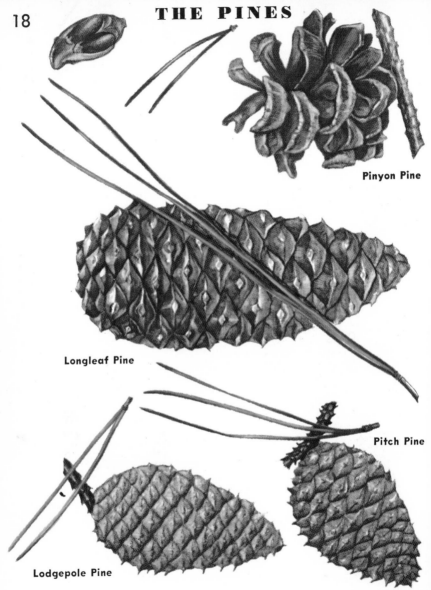

Pinyon Pine

Longleaf Pine

Pitch Pine

Lodgepole Pine

PINES are widely distributed conifers, most common in cool temperate regions. Conifers lack true flowers; the seeds develop in cones. The conifers include nearly 500 species in five families. Of these, the Pine family is largest

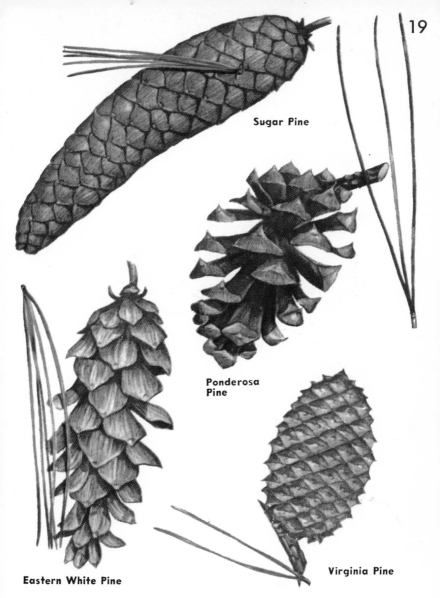

Sugar Pine

Ponderosa Pine

Eastern White Pine

Virginia Pine

and best known. It includes Spruce, Fir, Hemlock, and others besides those we commonly call Pines. True Pines have long needles, usually growing two to five in a cluster. The cones are large and well formed.

EASTERN WHITE PINE is a hardy and valuable north-eastern conifer. Prized for its timber, it was cut ruthlessly for years. Few prime stands of White Pine remain. New plantings are slowed by several diseases. One is the white pine blister rust, a fungus disease that spreads to White Pine from currants and gooseberries. Recognize White Pine by its soft, blue-green needles, five in a cluster. Cones are long and narrow, with thin, rounded scales; bark, dark with deep cracks; wood, light and soft. Western White Pine is somewhat similar; needles heavier, cones larger and longer.

Height: 50 to 100 ft. Pine family

SUGAR PINE, one of the tallest, largest, and most majestic of Pines, has a straight, tapering trunk topped by a flattened crown. The thick branches spread at almost right angles to the trunk. Needles, growing five in a cluster, are heavy, blue-green, with white tinge. They persist for two or three years. Cones, maturing in two years, are the largest known—12 to 15 in. long, often longer. The seeds are an important wildlife food. The bark is brown, with scaly ridges. The sugary sap crystallizes at cuts into white, crisp granules. The wood is reddish brown, light, and soft.

Height: 200 to 220 ft. Pine family

PITCH PINE prefers rocky, sandy regions and is tolerant of poor soil. Young trees on open ground may be rounded and symmetrical; older trees develop picturesque and irregular crowns of gnarled branches. As the name indicates, these Pines are rich in pitch or resin, which makes small branches and cones fine for torches or campfires. The gummy timber is brittle, of low grade, and of little economic value. Needles are in groups of three, 3 to 5 in. long, stiff and yellowish-green. The bark is reddish-brown, furrowed. The prickly, stemless cones persist on the trees for several years.

Height: 40 to 70 ft. Pine family

LONGLEAF PINE has, as its name implies, long needles —12 to 18 in. long, dark green and shiny, three in a cluster. The young shoots are a delight to the eye. Young Longleafs are cut for Christmas greens. Older trees are tapped for gums that produce turpentine, resin, and other "naval stores." Tapping may not injure the trees, which yield excellent all-purpose lumber. But the resin-covered cuts in the trees catch fire easily, making the forest dangerous in dry weather. The bark is orange-brown and scaly. Cones are 5 to 10 in. long, dull brown and spined.

Height: 100 to 120 ft. Pine family

PONDEROSA PINE also has long (4 to 7 in.) needles in clusters of three. It is a western tree, often growing larger than Longleaf Pine. Ponderosa, also called Western Yellow Pine, is prized for its lumber. Now the most widely used Pine for building, fencing, railroad ties, and construction, it is carefully cut to insure future supplies. Bark on young trees is dark brown, furrowed. Older trees develop large, flat, reddish plates. The brown cones, 3 to 5 in. long, with spiked scales, grow on short stalks. Young shoots, when broken, have an odor like that of an orange.

Height: 80 to 200 ft. Pine family

LODGEPOLE PINE has a dual personality. In open areas of the Rockies it is a thin, tall Pine, favored by the Indians for making poles for tipis and lodges. This form of Lodgepole Pine gave the tree its common name. But high in the mountains or along the shores, winds twist these Pines into gnarled, bent shapes that have earned for them the Latin name *contorta*. Many cones on this Pine hang for years without opening. However, fire—very destructive to this thin-barked Pine—causes the cones to open reseeding the burned area. The two needles are short and twisted.

Height: 15 to 80 ft. Pine family

VIRGINIA PINE is best known as a low, scrubby tree of waste places and abandoned farmlands. Also known as Jersey Pine, it predominates in the New Jersey pine barrens. On sandy, easily eroded land it provides cover under which more valuable trees may get started. The short, twisted, dull needles and sharp, prickly cones are characteristic. In northern states and Canada, the somewhat similar Jack Pine occurs. Its two needles are shorter, and the twisted cone is smoother. Virginia Pine has little value as timber, though it is occasionally used for pulp.

Virginia Pine

Height: 30 to 40 ft. Pine family

PINYON PINE produces the delicious pinyon or pine nuts, an Indian and wildlife delicacy, which we too have learned to enjoy. The low, drought-resistant tree grows on mesas and mountainsides in the Southwest. Its needles are short and stiff, in clusters of twos and threes. The wood is used for fenceposts and fuel. In late fall the Navajos and other Indians shake the nuts—which are large, wingless seeds—loose from the open cones, gathering them by the bushel. Another Pinyon Pine with about the same range has its needles singly instead of in twos or threes.

Height: 15 to 50 ft. Pine family

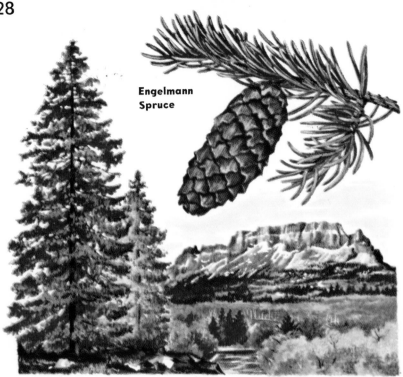

Engelmann
Spruce

SPRUCES grow straight and tall, tapering upward to a point. The branches are horizontal, often drooping. Since the wood is soft, fairly strong, and often free from knots, Spruce is a valuable timber tree. The wood is used in many kinds of construction and building. Canadian Spruce supplies much of our pulpwood. All Spruces can be recognized by their needles, arranged in compact spirals around the twigs. Each needle is four-sided, nearly square in cross-section. The cones, always hanging down, mature in one season. Eastern Spruces (Red, White, and Black) make up much of the cool northern forests. Southward they follow the higher parts of the Alleghenies.

Black Spruce

White Spruce

Red Spruce

Spruce Needle

Cross Section

Western Spruces are larger and include more species. The Blue Spruce is often planted as an ornamental (as is Norway Spruce, a European tree, with drooping branches and long cones). Of the western Spruces, Engelmann and Blue are most common. Sitka Spruces of the Northwest become giants 150 to 180 ft. high and 8 to 12 ft. thick. Spruces are used by northern wildlife during the long winter: spruce grouse and varying hares eat the needles, deer browse on the twigs, and crossbills, chickadees, and other songbirds feed on the small winged seeds.

Western

Eastern

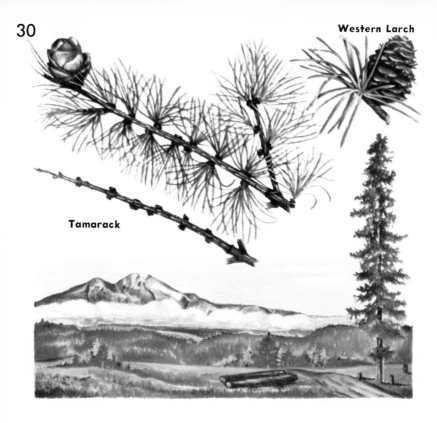

Western Larch

Tamarack

LARCHES or Tamaracks are northern conifers which, like the Baldcypress of the South, shed their leaves with the coming of winter. The slender, dark needles, about an inch long, grow in tufts of a dozen or more at the ends of stunted branchlets. The small, scaly cones are upright. Three species of Larch grow in this country; all are somewhat similar in appearance. The wood of these tall, straight trees is used for poles, lumber, and construction. The tough fibers from the roots of Tamarack were used by some eastern Indians to bind seams of their birchbark canoes.

Height: 50 to 120 ft. Pine family

DOUGLAS-FIR and its close relative, Bigcone Spruce, are not Firs or Spruces, but close relatives of Hemlock (p. 35). Like it, they have flat, soft, short-stalked needles, growing in a flattened spiral around the twig. The reddish cones, 2 to 3 in. long, have narrow, three-pointed bracts between the scales. Next to the Giant Sequoias, Douglas-fir with its rounded, straight, regular trunk is our largest tree. Some grow over 200 ft. high, but 100 ft. is more common. The wood varies from coarse to fine-grained. It yields plywood, construction timbers, and other lumber.

Height: 80 to 120 ft. Pine family

White Fir

FIRS are another group of northern conifers. Of about 25 species, 10 are found in the United States. All are tall, symmetrical, cone-shaped trees with dense branches. The smooth bark of young trees is broken by blisters of resin or balsam. The bark of older trees is furrowed or ridged. Fir needles are without stalks, generally flattened or grooved above. They are usually blunt-tipped and leave circular scars when they drop off. The cones are upright and long, and vary in color from green or purplish to brown. In the Northeast, the Balsam Fir is common. This spreading Fir is recognized by its smooth, even cones and by the whitish lines on the underside of the

Balsam Fir

needles. Fragrant, springy, Balsam boughs are used in making beds by many campers in the North Woods. More important is the resin obtained by cutting the bark. This resin, used for mounting microscopic specimens in laboratories, is known as Canada Balsam. White, California Red, Pacific Silver, Grand, and other species of Fir are found in our western mountains and up into Canada. Of 20 to 25 million Christmas trees cut each year, about 30 per cent are Balsam Fir. Douglas-fir ranks second, with other species of Fir and Spruce trailing.

Height: 50 to 200 ft. Pine family

Giant Sequoia

Redwood

Redwood
Giant Sequoia

Giant Sequoia

Giant Sequoia

REDWOOD and **GIANT SEQUOIA,** closely related trees, were once common, even in the arctic. Redwood, with leaves suggesting Hemlock, is the tallest tree (record: 364 ft.). Wood reddish, soft, and brittle. Giant Sequoia, with leaves like Juniper, is the largest and oldest living thing. Wood coarse, brown and brittle. Range limited; now protected in National Parks. General Sherman tree is 273 ft. high, 115 ft. around, and over 3,000 years old.

Height: 200-300 ft..Pine family

HEMLOCK, with its coarse wood, was ignored when the prime eastern forests were cut over. Now it has become an acceptable timber tree, used for construction, boxing, and pulpwood. Hemlocks are easily transplanted and are widely used in ornamental hedges. The bark is rich in tannin. Short, flat needles on minute stalks, in two flattened rows, are characteristic of Hemlock. These needles are darker above and silver-lined below. There are two eastern and two western species of Hemlock. The western ones, most common in the Northwest, are larger.

Height: 60 to 100 ft. Pine family

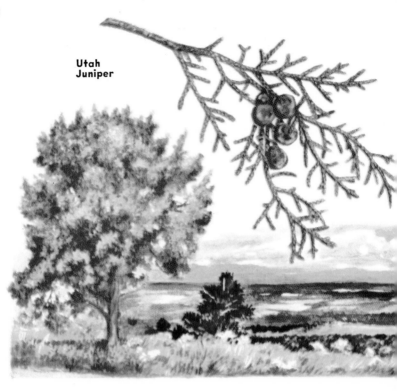

Utah
Juniper

JUNIPERS are found on rocky, sandy, or other poor soils in most parts of this country. They are most important in the West. Nine of our twelve species are found in the Far West. Most Junipers have minute, blunt, scaly leaves growing close to the twig. The fruit is a modified cone, with fleshy scales merging to form a bluish "berry" containing one or several seeds. Juniper berries are an important food of some birds and other small wildlife; many Indians like them too. The berry of the Common Juniper furnishes the flavor of gin. Junipers are generally stout, spreading trees, with thin, scaly, or fibrous bark. The Utah Juniper, a typical tree of the dry Southwest, is

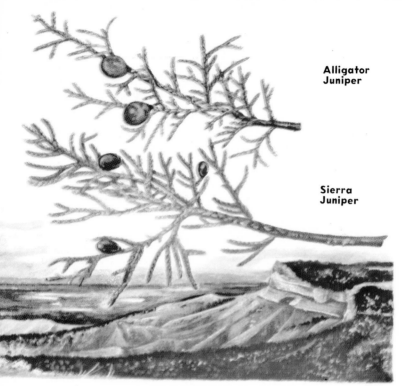

Alligator Juniper

Sierra Juniper

also called Desert Juniper. Its twigs are slender, and the round berry has a single seed. The berry, either fresh or dried, is used by local Indians in flavoring their food. The Alligator Juniper differs in having its thick gray bark broken into squared plates like that of the reptile's skin. Western Junipers are common in the same range as Pinyon Pines (p. 27) and are equally resistant to drought. The wood is used for fuel, lumber, ornaments, and fence-posts. No one will forget the pungent smell of burning Juniper in a camp-fire under western desert skies.

Height: 15 to 60 ft. Pine family

Nine Western Junipers

EASTERN RED-CEDAR is a Juniper, like those on pp. 36-37. It is a well-known tree of roadsides, fields, hedgerows. The leaves of Red-cedar are sharp and needle-like on young shoots, scaly on older twigs. The fruit is a purplish berry. The reddish wood is used for chests, pencils, posts, and shingles. Cedar oil, distilled from leaves and wood, is used in household preparations. Along the Gulf and in Florida, Southern Red-cedar, a related species, has smaller berries and thinner, drooping twigs. The name Cedar may be confusing, as it is used for several conifers not closely related.

Height: 20 to 60 ft. Pine family

NORTHERN WHITE-CEDAR is closely related to Western Red-cedar, a giant conifer of the Pacific Northwest. The White-cedar's twigs and short, light green, scale-like leaves are flattened into fan-like sprays. The brownish cones are very small. In contrast to the Junipers, these Cedars prefer moist or swampy soil. Varieties have been cultivated and grown for windbreaks and ornamental use. The smooth, resistant wood is used for shingles and siding. An eastern coastal species has smaller, narrower leaves.

Western Red-cedar

Northern White-cedar

Height: 25 to 50 ft. (Northern White-cedar, east); 100 to 150 ft. (Western Red-cedar, west). Pine family

BALDCYPRESS, like the Larches, sheds its leaves in the fall. This tall, pyramidal tree prefers moist or wet soils. It thrives in southeastern swamps, where conical "knees" grow up from the roots. These may aid in providing air for submerged parts. The leaves are flattened, soft, light green, and feathery, resembling Hemlock. The fruit is a small, dark, rounded cone. The durable wood, very resistant to rotting, is prized for posts, flats for nursery plants, ties, and construction. Baldcypress is planted as an ornamental, both here and in Europe, wherever winters are mild.

Height: 80 to 100 ft. Pine family

BLACKGUM, Sourgum, Pepperridge, and Tupelo are various names by which this handsome, medium-sized tree is known. It is common along moist roadsides and in woods. Of several southeastern species of Tupelo, two grow in swamps. One has large red fruit, from which preserves are made. Blackgum leaves (2 to 5 in. long) are smooth and shiny, turning brilliant red in fall. The dark blue fruit is eaten by birds and small mammals. A characteristic feature of Blackgum is the stiff horizontal twigs and branches. Sweetgum (p. 113) is not a relative, despite its name.

Height: 50 to 75 ft. Dogwood family

PERSIMMONS are common in warmer regions, where nearly 200 species are known. Only two are found in our country. One of these is confined to Texas. The Common Persimmon, a slender attractive tree of roadside, hedgerow, and open field, is especially plentiful in the South. In the fall the glossy green leaves become tinged with yellow, and some trees are laden with dull orange fruits. Male and female flowers are borne on separate trees, so only the latter bear fruit. The astringent fruit, edible after frost, is popular with opossums, raccoons, and foxes.

Height: 40 to 60 ft. Ebony family

DOGWOODS There are 17 American species of Dogwood, ranging from the tiny northern Bunchberry to the Pacific Dogwood, which may grow as high as 80 ft. Other species are shrubby or are small trees. Oppositely-placed, simple leaves with curved, almost parallel veins are field marks for the Dogwood group. The slow-growing Flowering Dogwood is best known, both in its wild and cultivated forms; the latter include pink-flowered varieties. The "flower" is a group of enlarged bracts around a cluster of small true flowers. The red fruits are as attractive as the flowers, and serve as food for wildlife as well. The dense, compact, fine-grained wood of Flowering Dogwood is unequaled for the making of shuttles for weaving. (Plate on p. 44.)

Height: 10 to 80 ft. Dogwood family

CATALPA (plate on p. 45) has become increasingly common and better known as it has been planted more and more outside of its original range. It is a handsome ornamental sometimes used in street planting. Two species of Catalpa grow in the United States, but the family to which they belong is prominent in the tropics and includes some 500 trees, shrubs, and vines. The large, heart-shaped leaves, spotted white flowers, and bean-like seed pods characterize Catalpa. The bark is red-brown and scaly. Leaves grow opposite or in threes. Catalpa is fast-growing. Its wood is coarse but durable, hence valuable for fences, posts, poles, and similar uses. Attempts have been made, with some success, to grow it as a wood crop.

Height: 20 to 50 ft. Bignonia family

FLOWERING DOGWOOD (text on p. 43)

CATALPA (text on p. 43)

REDBUDS once seen in bloom on a lawn or in a garden will always be recalled with delight. The wood is of no commercial value, but these small trees are favorite ornamentals, since they begin blooming when very young. They are hardy and colorful. In early spring the tree is a mass of lavender. The pale green, bean-like pods that follow the flowers become purple in late summer. The thin, heart-shaped leaves turn bright yellow in fall. The deep brown bark is smooth on young trees, furrowed on older ones. Redbud grows along streams and is tolerant of shade.

Height: 10 to 30 ft. Legume family

OSAGE-ORANGE like Catalpa is planted widely outside its original range. It was used as one of the first "living fences" to bound prairie farms. Indians prized the tough wood for bows and war clubs; we use it to a limited extent for posts and ties. Osage-orange is a relative of the Mulberries (pp. 114-115) and the Fig. It is easily identified by its shiny leaves, thorny twigs, bright orange inner bark. The unusual, wrinkled, orange-like fruit, 4 to 5 in. in diameter, has a typical citrus odor, but the inside is dry and pulpy, with a milky juice. It grows from a ball of small green flowers.

Height: 15 to 50 ft. Mulberry family

Original range

Umbrella Magnolia

Sweetbay

MAGNOLIAS (text on pp. 50-51)

Cucumber Magnolia

Southern Magnolia

MAGNOLIAS (text on pp. 50-51)

UMBRELLA MAGNOLIA is so called because large (12 to 20 in.), smooth, bright green leaves surround each flower like an umbrella. The compact tree, preferring rich, moist soils, develops a rounded, irregular crown. Branches are thick, twigs at sharp angles. Bark is gray,

thin, becoming warty. Flowers (4 to 8 in. across), creamy white, like larger Magnolias smell slightly unpleasant. Fruit reddens on ripening. (Plate on p. 48.)

Height: 20 to 30 ft. Magnolia family

SWEETBAY grows farther north along the Atlantic Coastal Plain than other Magnolias. In the North these trees are shrublike, but in southern swamps they sometimes grow 75 ft. high. Sweetbay is often planted as an ornamental in European gardens. The flower, small for Magnolias, is white and fragrant. Leaves are small, too

(3 to 6 in. long); bright green above, silvery white below. They drop late the next spring in the South, sometimes earlier in the North. Bark is gray, smooth and thin. (Plate on p. 48.)

Height: 30 to 50 ft. Magnolia family

CUCUMBER MAGNOLIA is one of the largest and hardiest of the six species of our native Magnolias. It has light brown, scaly bark, becoming thick and furrowed on older trees. The leaves—6 to 10 in. long, thin, light green, hairy below—typify the Cucumber Magnolia Buds are large, silky, pointed; flowers greenish-yellow, unat-

tractive. Fruits, like small cucumbers when immature, swell and open to reveal red seeds. (Plate on p. 49.)

Height: 50 to 80 ft. Magnolia family

SOUTHERN MAGNOLIA—or just "Magnolia"—is the name given to this very handsome tree, now used extensively as an ornamental. This large Magnolia, with thick branches and twigs, prefers the rich, moist soil of swamps and river banks, though it is adaptable under cultivation. Its Latin name, *Magnolia grandiflora*, testifies to the fact that it bears large flowers, 6 to 8 in. across. These white, waxlike flowers with a strong, heady fragrance, are all the more attractive by being set off by large, dark green, leathery leaves, 6 to 9 in. long, rusty-brown below. (Plate on p. 49.)
Height: 30 to 60 ft. Magnolia family

CULTIVATED MAGNOLIAS Our native Magnolias, widely used as ornamentals and for street planting in the South, are not hardy enough for planting in the North. Magnolias commonly seen in northern gardens are horticultural varieties from China and Japan, usually formed by crossing a hardy variety with a showy one. Even hardy cultivated Magnolias need sunny, protected places in the North. They usually bloom before their leaves come out; our native Magnolias bloom after. Their flowers are usually large, some up to 10 in. across; white, cream, or tinted with pink or lavender. Another half-dozen or more imported kinds, widely grown in the South, are tender species which need the same warm climate as our native Magnolias. Some, like native species, bloom after the leaves appear. Two have white flowers with a touch of red at the center. Some grow large; most are small trees or shrubs.

Cultivated Magnolia

PACIFIC MADRONE is an attractive, low-branching western tree common on slopes of Pacific coast ranges. It is a slow-growing, long-lived tree. The leathery, evergreen leaves, 3 to 5 in. long, shiny above and pale below, make a dense foliage. The brick-red bark is smooth, peeling in thin sheets from older trees. Flowers in white clusters give way to orange-red berries, which are eaten by pigeons and other birds. The brownish, brittle wood, which warps and checks badly in drying, has little use except in charcoal-making. Pacific Madrones include three species, and two of these species are rare.

Height: 20 to 50 ft. Heath family

CALIFORNIA-LAUREL or **BAY,** usually found in ravines and canyons, is a common evergreen tree of moist soils. The narrow, shiny, leathery leaves, 3 to 6 in. long, remain on the tree for two years or more. When crushed, they smell like camphor. The trunk often divides at its base. The bark is smooth, gray-brown, becoming scaly on older trees. The olive-like fruit, yellowish when ripe, has one large seed. Seeds are often washed down canyons and sprout to form dense thickets. The mottled, fine-grained wood is used in cabinetwork and for decorative effects.

Height: 20 to 50 ft. Laurel family

BLACK WILLOW is found along many streams in the eastern half of the country. Its irregular, spreading branches, large size, and dark trunk make it easy to recognize. The thin, narrow leaves often have stipules, like tiny heart-shaped collars at their base. They are the only willow leaves uniformly green on both sides. The flowers are in loose catkins, less fluffy than Pussy Willows. Male and female flowers, borne on separate trees, form small, hairy seeds. The soft, fine-grained wood is used to make artificial limbs; also for boxes, caning, and baskets.

Height: 30 to 60 ft. Willow family

WEEPING WILLOW, a native of China, was long ago introduced into Europe and the Middle East and later to this country. This is the Willow of the Bible, the one that grew by the waters of Babylon. It is widely cultivated where soil is moist, especially in cities, as it is tolerant of smoke and grime. Weeping Willow is now wild in some areas. The long, limp, pendent twigs are characteristic. The narrowly lance-shaped leaves, similar to those of other Willows, are 3 to 6 in. long. The minute seeds are covered with white hairs. The bark is grayish brown and fissured. Like other Willows, it is easily grown from stem cuttings.

Height: 20 to 50 ft. Willow family

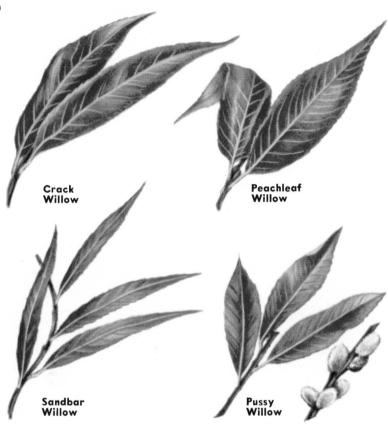

Crack Willow

Peachleaf Willow

Sandbar Willow

Pussy Willow

OTHER WILLOWS About 100 kinds of Willows grow in this country. Many are small and shrubby. Crack Willow, introduced from Europe, grows large. Twigs snap off, fall, and take root if the soil is moist. Sandbar Willow, sometimes large, more often forms riverside thickets. Note its very narrow leaves. Peachleaf Willow is more common on prairies along watercourses. Pussy Willow is a favorite in March and April, when opening buds mark a new growing season. It is cultivated for the flower market.

Peachleaf Willow

AMERICAN ELM is well known, because it is one of the conspicuous trees of eastern woods, fields, and town streets. Other Elms are found in Europe, Asia, and northern Africa. Widely planted, this Elm makes an excellent shade and street tree. Now it is menaced by insect pests and the Dutch Elm disease. The vase-shaped form and spreading, open branches make American Elm easy to identify at a distance. Note the uneven base and the double teeth on the leaf, and the smooth twigs. The wood is used for furniture, containers, and various small articles.

Height: 75 to 100 ft. Elm family

Winged Elm

Slippery Elm

WINGED AND SLIPPERY ELMS are both eastern trees, though the latter ranges farther north and west. Winged Elm or Wahoo has small leaves (1 to 3 in. long) and fruit. The corky outgrowths or wings on the twigs give it its name. The bark of Slippery Elm is brown and deeply furrowed. The inner bark of Slippery Elm twigs was formerly chewed for relief of throat ailments. The twigs are hairy but not corky. The fruit is large and flattened. Slippery Elm wood is similar to that of American Elm. Coarse, hard, and heavy, it makes fenceposts.

Height: 30 to 40 ft. (Winged); 40 to 60 ft. (Slippery). Elm family

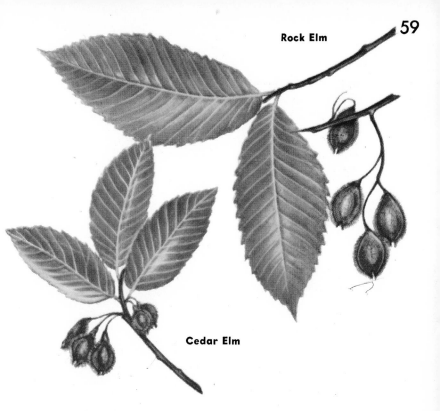

Rock Elm

Cedar Elm

ROCK AND CEDAR ELMS The hairy twigs of Rock Elm often have corky wings like those of Winged Elm. Rock Elm has larger fruit and generally grows farther north than Winged Elm. The leaves are larger, 3 to 6 in. long. Cedar Elm is at its best in the limestone hills of Texas. The thick, dark green leaves are smaller than those of any other native Elm (about the same size as the cultivated Siberian Elm). Its twigs are often corky; the bark is light brown and furrowed. This Elm, unlike others, flowers in late summer. The hairy seeds are similar to those of Rock Elm, but smaller.

Height: 50 to 70 ft. (both). Elm family

HACKBERRY, a relative of Elm, is readily recognized by its gray, warty bark and by the witches' brooms of tangled twigs caused by a fungus disease. There are eight species in this country and about fifty more the world over. Leaves are thinner than those of Elm, more pointed, and—in one Hackberry—less toothed. The small, hard fruits are eaten by wildlife, being a favorite of robins and mockingbirds. The wood—coarse, soft, and rather weak—is used occasionally for furniture and fencing, though Hackberry is primarily a shade and shelter belt tree.

Height: 5 to 80 ft. Elm family

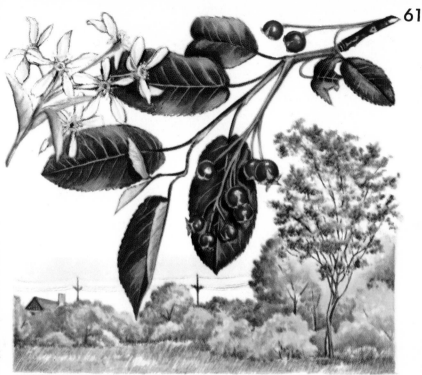

SERVICEBERRY or Shadbush is common over most of this country. Of some 20 species, most are western and shrubby. Only a few are trees. Serviceberries are found in woods, field borders, and roadsides. They do well in poor soil. The fruit, ripening early, is a favorite food of over 60 species of American wildlife, including many songbirds. Deer browse on the twigs. Serviceberry is identified by its finely saw-toothed, alternate leaves; grayish-brown, smooth bark; and, in spring, by its clusters of white, long-petaled flowers, opening early before the leaves are out.

Height: 15 to 50 ft. Rose family

AMERICAN HORNBEAM is known also as the Blue Beech because of its distinctive smooth, blue-gray, muscle-like bark. A low tree, it prefers moist soil along river banks, or low ground. The leaves are similar to the Hop Hornbeam's, but are smaller, darker, and more shiny. They turn orange and red in the fall. The fruits are clusters of nutlets in pairs, each set on a three-lobed bract. Songbirds use them as food. The light brown wood is tough, hard, and heavy. It is used for handles, wedges, and wherever hard wood is needed. The tree is planted as a moist-soil ornamental.
Height: 20 to 30 ft. Birch family

HOP HORNBEAM or Ironwood is related to American Hornbeam and is like it in some ways. Hop Hornbeam is mainly an upland tree, preferring open, well-drained woods. It grows taller and straighter than American Hornbeam, and is distinctive with its scaly, brown bark. The name refers to the hop-like fruits, which hang in compact clusters. Each seed is in a small bag formed from an inflated bract. The tough wood is used for tool handles, mallets, and the like. A smaller, western species is an unusually rare tree, found only in one Arizona locality.

Height: 20 to 40 ft. Birch family

AMERICAN HOLLY is the best known of a group of about 15 native Hollies, most of which are shrubby. American Holly, a plant of moist soil and river bottoms, reaches its best growth in the Southeast. It is widely planted where soil and climate are suitable. Recognize this Holly by its heavy, spiny, evergreen leaves and its smooth gray bark. Male and female flowers are borne on separate trees, and the bright red fruits only on the female tree. In winter and early spring they are a favorite food of songbirds, such as the bluebird, catbird and mockingbird.

Height: 20 to 50 ft. Holly family

AMERICAN BEECH is a stately and beautiful tree. Our native species is best known. Copper Beech and Weeping Beech are European varieties which are often planted as ornamentals in parks. Beech prefers rich bottomland or upland soils. It tolerates shade and gradually dominates the forest growth. Its distinctive smooth gray bark, long, pointed buds, and strongly veined leaves are characteristic. The fruit, a triangular nut, is eaten by mammals and birds. The wood—reddish, close-grained, and hard—is used for furniture, woodenware, barrel-making, and veneer.

Height: 60 to 80 ft. Beech family

Choke Cherry
10 to 20 ft.

Wild Black Cherry
40 to 80 ft.

WILD CHERRIES About 14 species of Wild Cherry, ranging from shrubs to large trees, are found in this country. All prefer moist soils on slopes and bottomlands. Larger Cherries are valued for their fine wood; all furnish

Pin Cherry
20 to 40 ft.

Wild Plum
10 to 20 ft.

fruits which are eaten avidly by wildlife, especially by song and game birds, bears, and many small mammals. Our cultivated Cherries come from Europe; the Flowering Cherries from Asia. Plums are close relatives.

Choke Cherry   **Wild Black Cherry**

CHOKE CHERRY is a shrub or small tree (10 to 20 ft. high) of irregular form. It is widely distributed throughout its range, forming thickets in dry, upland soil. Choke Cherry is a common constituent of hedgerows. On young trees the bark is smooth, gray, and spotted with narrow lenticels, like that of other Cherries. The leaves of Choke Cherry are shorter and more rounded than those of Black Cherry and come to an abrupt point. The fruits, in tight clusters, are dark red, astringent, and unpalatable when ripe. Birds eat them nevertheless. (Plate on p. 66.)

WILD BLACK CHERRY is the largest member of this group, growing 40 to 80 ft. high and occasionally higher. Its habit is always treelike. The tree spreads with age and develops drooping branches. Twigs are thin, with slender brown buds. The smooth, brownish bark on young trees becomes cracked into rough plates as the tree matures. Leaves are thick, narrow, tapering, and shiny green. Compared to other Cherries, this tree blooms late (in late May or June). Its clusters of small white flowers give way to

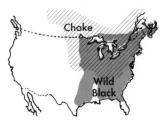

fruit, which become tart and black by the time they ripen. Songbirds do not let them hang for long. Cherry wood is valued for furniture and cabinetwork. (Plate on p. 66.)

Pin Cherry

Wild Plum

PIN CHERRY or Bird Cherry is a small slender tree of the East and North. It is a fast-growing tree, common on hillsides, in the mountains, and along field borders. Pin Cherry rarely grows more than 30 ft. high, with smooth, rusty brown bark marked with large lenticels. The small brown buds tend to cluster on the thin twigs. The leaves are even more narrow than Wild Black Cherry. They taper to a long point and are finely toothed. This tree is also called Red Cherry, since the fruits, eaten by many birds, are red when ripe. (Plate on p. 67.)

WILD PLUMS, some 16 species of them, are mostly shrubs. One becomes a small tree 10 to 20 ft. high, with short, thorny branches and twigs. Wild Plums form thickets throughout the Midwest. Early settlers counted on the fruit as part of their winter supply of preserves. Leaves of Wild Plums are more rounded and coarser-toothed than those of Cherries. The fruit is larger, grows singly instead of in clusters, and is orange or red when ripe. Though the fruits are more attractive to us, they are not eaten as much by wildlife as are the Wild Cherries. However, many birds and small mammals make plum thickets their favorite retreat. Foxes eat the fruit occasionally. (Plate on p. 67.)

Pin Cherry

Wild Plums

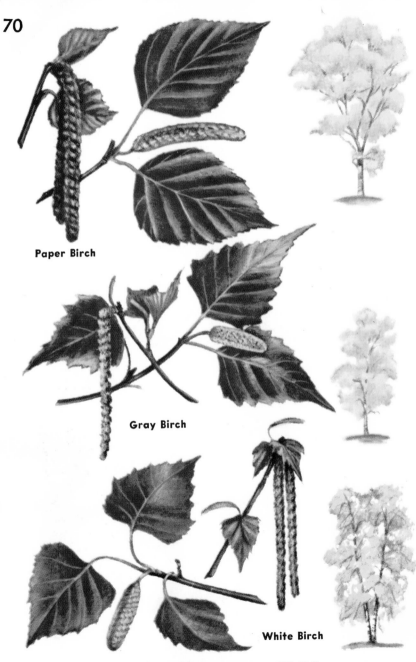

Paper Birch

Gray Birch

White Birch

BIRCHES (text on pp. 72-74)

Yellow Birch

River Birch

Sweet Birch

BIRCHES (text on pp. 72-74)

PAPER BIRCH or Canoe Birch is the White Birch of the North—the tree used by Indians to make their birchbark canoes. Its bark was also used to make baskets, dishes, and trays. Paper Birch is a tree of open woods and river-banks, common and well known throughout the North.

It grows tall (occasionally 100 ft.), with a rounded top and numerous large horizontal branches. Twigs are thin and droop slightly. The smooth, chalk-white bark is spotted with horizontal openings (lenticels). It becomes scaly with age. The leaves are oval, 2 to 4 in. long, coarsely toothed, darker above. (Plate on p. 70.)

Height: 50 to 70 ft. Birch family

GRAY BIRCH is often called White Birch, but this name confuses the tree with several others. This is a small north-ern tree, often growing in clusters or thickets. It never attains the stature of either our Paper Birch or the European White Birch, which it resembles mainly in the color of its bark. While its thin bark is something like that of Paper Birch, the triangular leaves are dis-tinctly different. Like all Birches, it bears fruit in a narrow cone with many small, winged seeds. Flowers are catkins. Wood—heavy, close-grained, and reddish-brown in color —is used for spools, clothespins, and hoops. (Plate on p. 70.)

Paper (red)   Gray (blue)

Height: 20 to 40 ft. Birch family

YELLOW BIRCH like Paper Birch is a northern or mountain tree with bark that eventually peels into thin, curly, silvery-yellow strips. It is one of the larger Birches, growing occasionally 100 ft. high, with rounded top and typical drooping twigs. Leaves are nearly oval, double-toothed, 3 to 4 in. long, paler below, with a wintergreen odor. Yellow Birch prefers rich open woods, well-drained soil. The wood of Yellow and similar Birches is good for furniture, woodenware, boxes, better plywood. (Plate on p. 71.)

Height: 50 to 75 ft. Birch family

RIVER BIRCH, or **RED BIRCH,** is the only Birch common in the South. It grows 50 to 80 ft. tall, with short, hanging branches and thin twigs. It prefers moist, swampy soil and river banks. The leaves, 1 to 3 in., double-toothed as in Yellow Birch, are more irregular, and more deeply indented, turning dull yellow in autumn. Flowers are catkins, 2 to 3 in. long, opening before the leaves. The bark, a warm, reddish-brown, curls into thin sheets on young trees and breaks into shallow plates on older trunks. The fruit, an erect cone similar to that of Yellow Birch, is somewhat more pointed. (Plate on p. 71.)

Height: 50 to 80 ft. Birch family

WHITE BIRCH is even more common in northern Europe than our Canoe Birch is here. During the early part of the century it was imported into this country as an ornamental and is still widely used for home and park plantings. White Birch is a spreading, short-lived tree with

drooping branches, somewhat like Gray Birch but with bark thicker, less smooth. From it Europeans made bowls, spoons, shoes, and brooms (from twigs). Among horticultural varieties, one has pendulous, willow-like branches; another, leaves deep-cut and divided. (Plate on p. 70.)

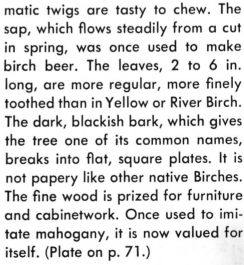

Height: 50 to 75 ft. Birch family

SWEET BIRCH, or Black or Cherry Birch, grows up to 75 ft. high. Graceful and symmetrical, it prefers rich,

well-drained upland soil. The aromatic twigs are tasty to chew. The sap, which flows steadily from a cut in spring, was once used to make birch beer. The leaves, 2 to 6 in. long, are more regular, more finely toothed than in Yellow or River Birch. The dark, blackish bark, which gives the tree one of its common names, breaks into flat, square plates. It is not papery like other native Birches. The fine wood is prized for furniture and cabinetwork. Once used to imitate mahogany, it is now valued for itself. (Plate on p. 71.)

Sweet Birch

Height: 40 to 60 ft. Birch family

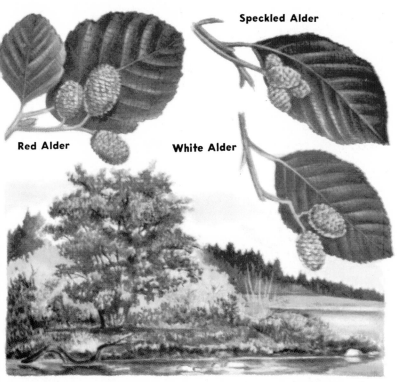

Speckled Alder

Red Alder

White Alder

ALDERS are close relatives of the Birches, with similar flowers, fruits, and seeds. Their bark is marked with horizontal lenticels as in Birches. Alders, however, are mostly shrubs. Of about nine species in this country, only two become good-sized trees: the Red and White Alders of the Pacific Coast. The short-stemmed, alternate leaves vary from species to species, but all are characterized by strong feather veins. Flowers are greenish or yellowish catkins. The fruits are small, woody cones. Alders are fast-growing and prefer moist soil along streams or in swamps.

Height: 20 to 80 ft. Birch family

SOURWOOD is an interesting tree related to the Pacific Madrone (p. 52). In late spring the rows of white, bell-shaped flowers add to its beauty. The simple, alternate leaves are shiny dark green, turning a rich scarlet with the coming of cold weather. Because of its attractive appearance, Sourwood is sometimes used as an ornamental, especially in the South. The name refers to the sour taste of the twigs, which are chewed by woodsmen as a thirst quencher. The bark is reddish gray, smooth at first, becoming scaly with age. The fruit is a small hairy capsule with many seeds.

Height: 15 to 40 ft. Heath family

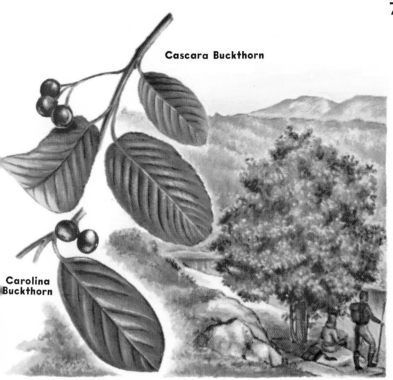

Cascara Buckthorn

Carolina
Buckthorn

BUCKTHORNS are widely distributed. Only a few of the 10 to 15 American species are treelike. All have simple leaves growing alternately on the twigs. In some, the leaves have smooth edges; in others they are finely toothed. The fruit, similar to that of Wild Cherry, is red or black when ripe. It is eaten by songbirds in the West and South. Woodpeckers are fond of the fruits; so are catbirds and mockingbirds. Buckthorns are too small to have timber value. Some are used as ornamentals. The bark of a western species produces cascara, a laxative drug.

Height: 15 to 25 ft. Buckthorn family.

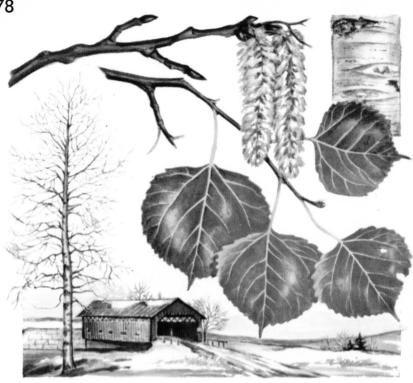

QUAKING ASPEN is one of the smaller Poplars and one of the best known. The simple, alternate, almost round leaves, on thin, flattened stalks, stir in the faintest breeze, giving the tree its name. The bark on young trees is a pale greenish white, becoming darker and rougher with age. Twigs are thick; buds waxy and scaly. Quaking Aspen is a quick-growing, upland tree of sandy or rocky soils and burnt-over land. It looks its best against the dark conifers in the Rockies. It is known also as Trembling or American Aspen. The soft, white wood is used for pulp, excelsior, matches.

Height: 20 to 40 ft. Willow family

BIGTOOTH ASPEN or Large-tooth Aspen is named for the large, rounded teeth on the margins of its heart-shaped leaves. It is a northeastern tree, similar in form and growth to Quaking Aspen, but with heavier twigs and larger, coarser leaves. As in other Poplars, the flower is a drooping catkin which opens before the leaves are out. The catkin develops into a cluster of fruits with small, hairy seeds that are easily distributed by the wind. All Poplars are quick-growing and produce a quick cover in burnt-over areas. The soft, light wood is used for pulp, boxes, excelsior, and matches.

Height: 30 to 60 ft. Willow family

COTTONWOODS are common, widely distributed Poplars which are appreciated most in their native open prairies, where they follow the watercourses. They are planted for shade near ranchers' homes, along streets, and as windbreaks. Cottonwoods are large trees with pale bark which becomes deeply furrowed on older trees. The twigs are heavy; the buds large, pointed, and gummy. The wood is used for lumber and boxes as well as pulp.

About a dozen species occur in this country, some with narrow, willow-like leaves, but most with leaves similar to those illustrated.

Height: 60 to 100 ft. Willow family

AMERICAN BASSWOOD or Linden, a handsome shade tree, spreads broadly when space permits. Several other species occur. Grayish-brown twigs bear plump, rounded winter buds. The large, heart-shaped, veiny leaves are easy to identify. Basswood bark is dark and deeply furrowed. European Lindens, with their smaller leaves and more compact crowns, are used in street planting. The wood of our species is light and fine-grained, used in woodenware, cabinetwork and for toys. The flowers, which yield an excellent honey, perfume the air on warm June nights.

Height: 60 to 100 ft. Linden family

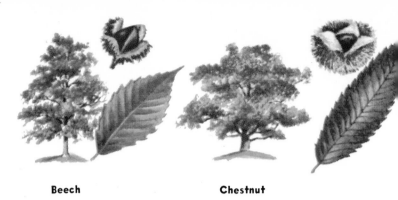

Beech

Chestnut

BEECH

COMPARISON OF WH

White
Oaks

Spring   Summer   Fall   Winter

Black
Oaks

THE OAKS rank with the world's most important trees.
Venerated by ancient peoples, they are still symbols of
strength. These members of the Beech family are related
to the once-common Chestnut. This important forest tree
was almost completely destroyed by a rampant fungus
disease; only a few scattered sucker growths remain.
Tanbark-oak resembles both Oak and Chestnut; it bears
acorns. Oaks make up one of the largest groups of native
trees in the United States. At least 50, perhaps 75, species
occur in this country, mainly in the East. They are our most
important hardwood timber for lumber, fuel, barrels, railroad ties, and other uses. All Oaks have the distinctive
fruit—the acorn. All have alternate simple leaves, some
entire and others toothed or lobed. Nearly all Oaks can

Tanbark-oak   Oaks

FAMILY

BLACK OAKS

Acorns Ripen
in One
Season

Spring   Summer   Fall   Winter

in Two
Seasons

be put in the White Oak or the Black Oak group. The White Oaks (pp. 84-95) mature their acorns in a single year; the leaves have rounded lobes and usually lack teeth; the bark is generally pale. The Black Oaks (pp. 96-107) take two years to mature acorns; leaves have sharper lobes and bristle-pointed teeth; the bark is usually dark. Some Oaks are hard to identify; use leaves, tree form, bark, buds, and acorns as guides. Oaks are important sources of food for many kinds of wildlife, and in years when the mast crop (acorns) fails, the deer, squirrels, and raccoons may have trouble finding enough to eat.

Ten species · Nine species · One species · Thirty-six species

WHITE OAK
5″ to 7″

POST OAK
4″ to 6″

BUR OAK
5″ to 7″

OVERCUP OAK
5″ to 7″

CHESTNUT OAK
6″ to 8″

CHINKAPIN OAK
4″ to 6″

SWAMP WHITE OAK
5″ to 7″

LIVE OAK
3″ to 4″

GAMBEL OAK
3″ to 5″

**CALIFORNIA
LIVE OAK**
2″ to 3″

POST OAK
1/2" to 1"

WHITE OAK
3/4" to 1"

OVERCUP OAK
1/2" to 1 1/2"

BUR OAK
3/4" to 2"

CHINKAPIN OAK
1/2" to 3/4"

CHESTNUT OAK
1" to 1 1/2"

LIVE OAK
3/4" to 1"

SWAMP WHITE OAK
3/4" to 1 1/2"

**CALIFORNIA
LIVE OAK**
3/4" to 1 1/2"

GAMBEL OAK
1/2" to 3/4"

WHITE OAK is the best known Oak of all. Common throughout New England, its beauty attracted the attention of early colonists. In open places White Oak develops a broad, symmetrical crown and majestic appearance. The light gray, scaly bark is characteristic; so are the leaves, with five to nine rounded lobes. Young opening leaves are pinkish or red, as are the leaves in autumn. White Oak prefers rich soil but grows slowly. The large, pointed acorns in shallow cups were eaten by Indians. It is an outstanding lumber tree, used for furniture, boats, and barrels.

Height: 60 to 120 ft. Beech family

POST OAK is smaller than White Oak but in open areas they both develop the same rounded form. Post Oak's bark is grayish, with broad, scaly ridges. The oblong leaves, clustered at ends of twigs, are thicker, hairy beneath, and more leathery than in White Oak. They have three to seven broad lobes, the middle ones being the largest. The leaf is wedge-shaped at its base. Occasionally trees with three-lobed leaves are found. The acorns are similar to White Oak, but smaller. The wood is used for rough construction, for railroad ties, and, as its name indicates, for posts.

Height: 40 to 60 ft. Beech family

BUR OAK has a top-heavy leaf, broad toward the tip and abruptly narrowed toward the center. The indentation or sinus sometimes cuts close to the midrib. The lower lobes are shallow, and the tapering leafbase is wedge-shaped. The scaly, hairy, deep cup of its large acorn gives this Oak its name. The cup covers about half the nut. The deeply furrowed bark is grayish-brown. Bur Oak is a rugged tree with thick spreading branches and an irregular, rounded crown. It prefers moist localities, but tolerates poor, dry soil in fields, along roadsides, and even in the prairies.

Height: 50 to 80 ft. Beech family

OVERCUP OAK compared to Bur Oak has a narrower leaf, which is more hairy beneath. Fall colors vary from yellow to red. The medium-sized acorns are almost entirely enclosed by the cup. They are smaller than the acorns of Bur Oak and lack the ragged fringe. Overcup is a medium-sized to large Oak, which is restricted to bottomlands and wet soil. Though widely distributed in the Southeast, it is not very common. The bark is like Bur Oak but darker. The wood — dark brown, hard, heavy, close-grained, and durable—is used and often marketed as White Oak.

Height: 50 to 70 ft. Beech family

CHESTNUT OAK is mainly a mountain tree of the Appalachians. It grows up to 100 ft. high with an irregular crown. Chestnut Oak thrives in dry, rocky soil, often on hillsides and ravines. Its dark brown bark, until recently harvested as a source of tanbark for tanning leather, is very deeply furrowed. The tree's name refers to its Chestnut-like leaf. But the leaf is broader and has rounded teeth, while that of Chestnut is more pointed and has sharp-pointed teeth. Acorns of Chestnut Oak often sprout in the fall, soon after dropping. The wood is hard, strong, and close-grained.

Height: 60 to 80 ft. Beech family

CHINKAPIN OAK has a leaf somewhat resembling that of Chestnut Oak, though it is slightly irregular, more narrow and more pointed. It is hairy beneath. Chinkapin Oak prefers richer soil than Chestnut Oak and grows over a much wider range. It extends, in isolated stands, as far west as New Mexico. The bark is like that of White Oak— gray and scaly. The acorns are smaller (½ in.) than in any closely related Oak. They are rounded and about half enclosed by their cup. The wood, like that of other White Oaks, is used in construction and for lumber. The name is Indian, meaning "large."

Height: 30 to 80 ft. Beech family

SWAMP WHITE OAK is an irregular, somewhat shaggy oak found in swamps and other moist areas. The bark, though gray, has more brown than in White Oak, and is ridged and scaly, even on twigs. The leaf edges are wavy rather than deeply lobed, and are hairy beneath. Swamp White Oak acorns are borne in pairs on a stalk, 2 to 4 in. long. Farther south, in the same kind of moist habitat, one finds the closely related Swamp Chestnut or Basket Oak. These and most other trees in the White Oak group do not develop brilliant autumn colors. Lumber from all is sold as White Oak.

Height: 60 to 80 ft. Beech family

LIVE OAK has become a symbol of the South. The low, spreading tree, often covered with Spanish Moss, marks old plantations and roadside plantings. The elliptical, blunt-tipped, leathery leaves are evergreen—that is, they remain green and on the tree throughout the year. The acorns are small but edible; wood is used for furniture. Two other southeastern Oaks (Laurel and Willow) have leaves of somewhat similar shape, but they are thinner and more pointed than Live Oak. Several western Oaks are evergreen. Botanists apply the unqualified name Live Oak only to this species.

Height: 40 to 60 ft. Beech family

GAMBEL OAK or Utah White Oak is common in the Rockies, where it is a shrub or small- to medium-sized tree. Thickets of Gambel Oak are common in high, dry places, where they offer shelter to deer and other wildlife. The leaf resembles that of White Oak but is thicker and hairy beneath. The scaly bark is grayish brown. The acorns are small, with the cup covering about a third of the nut. Other western White Oaks include the Oregon White Oak, with large rounded acorns, and the California White Oak, with very long pointed ones in a shallow cup.

Height: 20 to 70 ft. Beech family

CALIFORNIA LIVE OAK or Coast Live Oak is an attractive evergreen Oak found in open groves and as a shade tree. It is a broad tree with a low, spreading crown frequently branching near the ground. The Hollylike leaves are evergreen, tough, shiny green above and hairy below. They are oval or oblong, with short spiny teeth. The acorn is long and pointed, with a scaly cup (compare with Canyon Live Oak, p. 107). Blue Oak or Mountain White Oak has a longer and less toothed leaf, which is not evergreen. The rounded acorn is in a shallow cup.

Height: 30 to 50 ft. Beech family

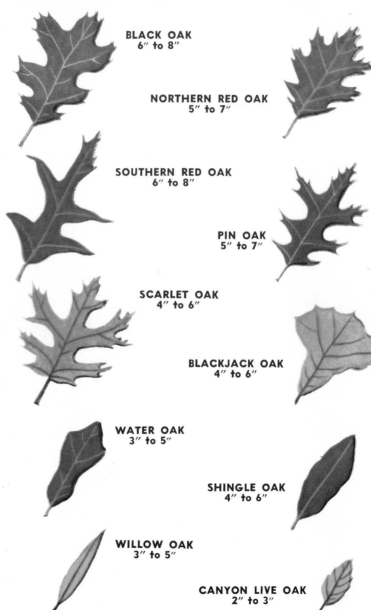

BLACK OAK
6" to 8"

NORTHERN RED OAK
5" to 7"

SOUTHERN RED OAK
6" to 8"

PIN OAK
5" to 7"

SCARLET OAK
4" to 6"

BLACKJACK OAK
4" to 6"

WATER OAK
3" to 5"

SHINGLE OAK
4" to 6"

WILLOW OAK
3" to 5"

CANYON LIVE OAK
2" to 3"

ACORNS

BLACK OAK
1/2" to 3/4"

NORTHERN RED OAK
1/2" to 1 1/4"

SOUTHERN RED OAK
1/2"

PIN OAK
1/4" to 1/2"

SCARLET OAK
1/2" to 3/4"

BLACKJACK OAK
3/4"

WATER OAK
1/4" to 3/4"

SHINGLE OAK
1/2" to 3/4"

WILLOW OAK
1/4" to 1/2"

CANYON LIVE OAK
1" to 2"

BLACK OAK is one of the most common eastern Oaks. It sets the pattern for Oaks with spiny leaves, dark bark, and acorns which take two years to ripen. Black Oak leaves are variable, dark and shiny with hairy veins. Those on the lower part of the tree are broader and have shallower lobes than the leaves higher on the trees. The orange inner bark is an important identifying characteristic even though you have to gouge with a knife to see it.

Acorns are medium-sized, with a broadly rounded, downy nut, about half enclosed in a deep cup. The wood is coarse, hard, and heavy.

Height: 60 to 90 ft. Beech family

NORTHERN RED OAK is a widespread, common Oak of open woods. It is one of the largest Oaks, occasionally 125 ft. high. Its dark bark has conspicuous long, smooth plates between the furrows. The leaves tend to hang vertically on the stalks, and the lobes tend to be more triangular than in other species. The leaves are smooth or only lightly hairy along the veins. The middle lobes are largest. Acorns are large and rounded in a shallow cup. Red Oak, with its close-grained, reddish-brown wood, is regarded as the most important timber tree of the Black Oaks. It is also a shade tree.

Height: 60 to 90 ft. Beech family

SOUTHERN RED OAK is often called Spanish Oak. There are two principal strains: one with three-lobed leaves, the other with leaves having five deep lobes. Some of the three-lobed leaves are almost triangular. Both kinds have tapering, wedge-shaped bases, and are rusty or hairy beneath. The dark bark furrows into narrow ridges. The acorns are small (½ in. long) and rounded, in shallow, scaly cups. The brown, coarse wood is valuable for flooring, construction, and millwork. In the Southeast this Oak is often planted for shade and as an ornamental tree.

Height: 70 to 80 ft. Beech family

PIN OAK takes its name from the many short, pinlike twigs that clutter the horizontal or downward-sloping branches. These make identification easy in winter. The leaf has five to seven deep lobes with long teeth; it is dark green above, lighter and smooth below. The gray-brown bark remains smooth for some time, gradually breaking into scaly ridges. Pin Oak is partial to moist soil. It is a hardy tree, widely used in street and ornamental planting. Pin Oak is widely culti-vated in Europe. Acorns are small (about ½ in. long), rounded, with a shallow cup.

Height: 70 to 80 ft. Beech family

SCARLET OAK is so called because of the brilliant color of its autumn leaves. It is a common, robust, tapering, open-crowned tree of forest and roadside, preferring dry, sandy soils. The dark bark is strongly fissured. The leaf, 3 to 6 in. long, is smooth, shiny, with few or no hairs below, somewhat resembling Pin Oak. However, it is larger than that of Pin Oak, with five to seven deep lobes. The sinuses between them are broadly rounded. The acorn, medium-sized, is about half covered by a deep cup. The reddish-brown wood, though coarse and heavy, is sometimes sold as Red Oak.

Height: 70 to 80 ft. Beech family

BLACKJACK OAK is a small tree, growing in well-drained sandy soil and wastelands. The leaves, 3 to 7 in. long, are coarse and leathery, dark green above, covered below with brownish hair and turn dull yellow or brown in the fall. Their broad, rounded tip, shallow lobes, and short leafstalks are characteristic, though the shape of the leaf is somewhat variable. Blackjack acorns are small, about half enclosed in a cup. The bark is black, thick, rough, and broken into nearly square plates. The wood is of very limited value and is used mainly for fuel or charcoal.

Height: 20 to 30 ft. Beech family

WATER OAK is a common southern Oak; a tree of riverbanks, marshes, and flood plains. It is sometimes planted as a southern shade tree. Despite its name, it also grows in dryer woods with other Oaks, Hickories, Ash, and Gum. Leaves are somewhat similar to those of Blackjack Oak but smaller (2 to 5 in. long), thinner, narrower, and with less hair beneath. They are a dull blue-green, turning yellow in the fall. The bark is dark gray, smooth when young, later becoming broken into irregular ridges. The acorn, small and broadly rounded; usually has two distinct color zones.

Height: 50 to 80 ft. Beech family

SHINGLE OAK is a handsome tree with slender branches and a tall, pyramidal, rounded crown. It resembles Willow Oak but has broader, coarser leaves. Leaves (3 to 6 in. long) are dark green above, paler and hairy beneath, with wavy margins and a spiny tip. They look as if they should be evergreen, but are not. A few of the autumn leaves turn dull brown and hang on the twigs all winter. The bark is dark brown, smooth, becoming deeply cracked with age. The wood is hard and heavy. Acorns are small, somewhat flattened, and about half covered by a reddish-brown, scaly cup.

Height: 50 to 60 ft. Beech family

WILLOW OAK has small leaves shaped like the Willows, but here the similarity ends. The leaves are fairly thick, blunt, lack teeth, and have a smooth edge. They are shiny green above, paler beneath. The straight trunk and numerous side branches are characteristic of this Oak. The medium-sized Willow Oak is widely planted and has become a popular shade tree in the South. It prefers rich, moist soil. The acorns, growing on very short stalks, are small and rounded, in shallow cups. The wood is reddish brown, similar to wood of other Black Oaks but of somewhat inferior quality.

Height: 50 to 90 ft. Beech family

CANYON LIVE OAK has acorns ripening in two years; the somewhat similar California Live Oak (p. 95) acorns ripen in one. Both are low, spreading trees, but the more variable leaves of Canyon Live Oak have a yellowish fuzz beneath. Some have coarse teeth; some are nearly smooth. Canyon Live Oak is a small tree (occasionally up to 100 ft. tall) of hillsides and mountain valleys. Several shrubby forms have been described. Acorns vary in size and form, but have a thick, yellowish, wooly cup. California Live Oak has long pointed acorns.

Height: 40 to 50 ft. Beech family

SASSAFRAS, called Green Stick by the Indians because of its bright green twigs, is a common eastern tree or shrub with peculiar, mitten-shaped, three-lobed leaves. Some are entire, a few have two lobes, but all turn a rich orange and red in the autumn. Children chew the aromatic twigs. Older people recall the teas and tonics made from Sassafras roots. Birds, including quail, feed on the purple fruits. The warm brown bark of older trees is deeply furrowed. Sassafras grows along roadsides and fencerows, and in open fields, in well-drained, acid soils.

Height: 25 to 50 ft. Laurel family

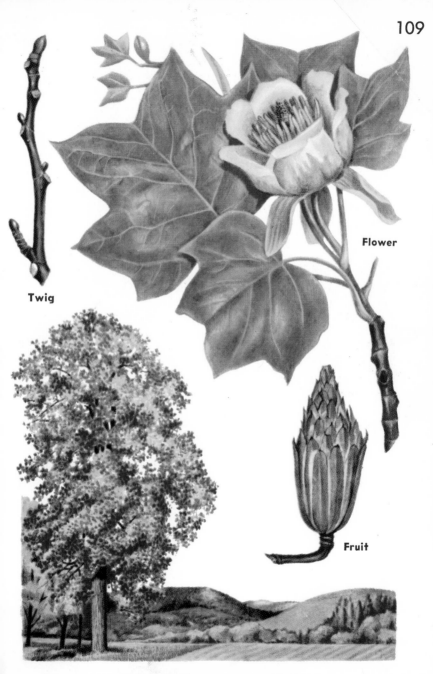

Twig

Flower

Fruit

TULIPTREE (text on p. 110)

TULIPTREE or Yellow-poplar is a tree of ancient lineage. Closely related to the primitive Magnolias (pp. 48-51), the Tuliptrees go back over fifty million years. Fossil leaves have been found in rocks of Europe and Greenland. The Tuliptree grows tall, its straight trunk free of branches near the ground. A beautiful tree in all seasons, it is planted as an ornamental but not as a shade tree. The peculiar squarish leaves, broad and notched, make identification easy. The tree is named from the greenish-yellow tulip-like flowers, opening in May and June. Buds, closed by two purse-like scales, are unique. The fruit is a cone of many small, winged seeds. The bark is thick, grayish, ridged. The creamy yellow wood, soft, easily worked, is used for pulp and manufactured articles. (Plate on p. 109.)

Height: 80 to 120 ft. Magnolia family

HAWTHORNS or Haws are a thorn in the botanist's side. Their identification and classification are complex. Some authorities set the number of American species at 165; others at over 1,200. While species such as Scarlet Haw (p. 112) are distinct enough to be recognized without much difficulty, it is generally sufficient to identify one of these trees as "a Hawthorn." Hawthorns are small trees or shrubs, some with irregular, thorny branches. The smooth, brownish bark breaks into thin, scaly plates with age. Hawthorn leaves are simple, toothed, and sometimes lobed, alternating on the twigs. The flowers are

white or pink, in clusters. Fruits, like miniature apples, are orange, yellow, or red, and not as valuable to wildlife as appearance suggests.

Height: 10 to 25 ft. Rose family

Ashe Hawthorn

English Hawthorn

Little Hip
Hawthorn

Cockspur Haw

HAWTHORNS (text on pp. 110 and 112)

SCARLET HAW is one of the more common eastern Hawthorns. It is an attractive tree which is also cultivated as an ornamental. This Haw is a small tree with many straight thorns, an inch or so long. The leaf is toothed, with small, rounded lobes. Flowers appear in May and develop into hanging fruit, first green and downy, becoming red in fall. The bark is thin, gray, and scaly. Scarlet Haw is a tree of dry soils, found in fencerows, old fields, and open woods. It and other Hawthorns provide some food and a lot of thorny, protective shelter for songbirds and other wildlife.

Height: 15 to 20 ft. Rose family

SWEETGUM, also called Liquidamber, is often planted as a shade tree because of brilliant fall coloring in its foliage. It is a tall, straight tree of low, moist places. Its short, gray, horizontal branches bear thick twigs with corky ridges. The star-shaped leaves are somewhat like those of Maple but grow alternate on the twigs. The hanging, dry fruit, a ball covered with tiny horns, opens to release small winged seeds, which are eaten by birds. The bark is thick, gray, and scaly. The soft, weak, brownish wood is used for furniture, cabinetwork, and veneer.

Height: 80 to 120 ft. Witch Hazel family

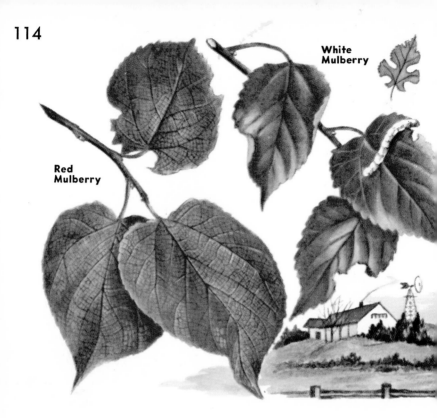

White Mulberry

Red Mulberry

MULBERRIES are small or medium-sized trees closely related to Hackberry (p. 60) and Osage-orange (p. 47). The leaves and twigs yield a milky juice. We have native and imported species. The leaves of all are alternate, heart-shaped or lobed, with small, blunt teeth. The Red Mulberry, native and common throughout the East, gave early settlers hope of establishing a silk industry in this country. It is a tree of roadsides and bottomlands. The leaves, in contrast to those of White Mulberry, are somewhat hairy beneath and rough. The berry-like fruit, ripe in midsummer, is a purplish red. Red Mulberry is sometimes planted as a shade tree. White Mulberry is a somewhat similar tree from Asia. It was brought from China

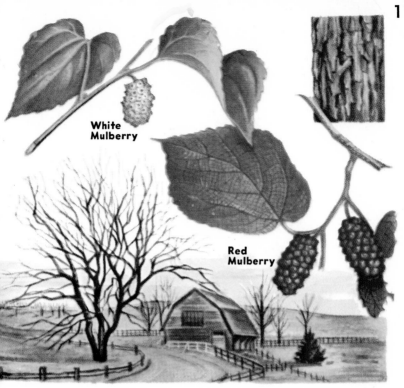

White Mulberry

Red Mulberry

and Japan in an effort to start an American silk industry. White Mulberry has smooth leaves and whitish or lavender fruit. These, and the fruit of Red Mulberry, are favorites of songbirds. The Black Mulberry from Persia is sometimes cultivated in the warmer parts of this country. It has large, dark-colored fruits. Paper-mulberry is an oriental species planted as an ornamental in the South, where it occasionally escapes and becomes naturalized. The leaves are very rough and hairy, lobed or entire, 3 to 8 in. long. In China and Japan paper was made from its inner bark.

Height: 30 to 50 ft. Mulberry family

Red Mulberry

Sugar
Maple

Black Maple

Mountain Maple

Silver
Maple

MAPLES, next to Oaks, are the best-known broad-leaved trees. Maples have world-wide distribution in temperate lands. Some 60 to 80 species are known; about a quarter of them are found in North America. Some are shrubby,

Norway Maple

Red Maple

Broadleaf Maple

Rocky Mountain Maple

but most are medium to large trees. All have palm-shaped, simple, opposite leaves, except Boxelders (p. 138). Their typical paired, winged fruits are eaten by birds, by squirrels, and by other small animals.

NORWAY MAPLE is the tree sometimes mistaken for Sugar Maple. This tree, of European origin, is commonly planted along city streets because of its resistance to smoke, dust, and insect pests. While the leaf is somewhat similar to that of Sugar Maple, it is broader—usually wider than it is long. Norway Maple is a medium-sized, fast-growing tree, developing a rounded crown and dense foliage. The greenish-yellow flowers, in drooping clusters, and the winged seeds which develop from them are large for Maples. Norway Maple yields a milky juice when fruit or leaf stem is broken. Sugar Maple does not. One variety of Norway Maple has purplish leaves.

Height: 40 to 70 ft. Maple family

SUGAR MAPLE needs no introduction. Everyone knows of its sugary sap, from which maple syrup and maple sugar are made. But, in addition, Sugar Maple is a fine shade and ornamental tree used for street and home plantings. The wood is excellent for furniture, cabinet-work, and wood turning. Its leaves, with straight-sided lobes, are not so wide or thick as those of Norway Maple. The teeth are large and few in number. Leaves turn a rich yellow, orange, or scarlet in fall. The gray bark forms plates which become flaky with age. The fruit ripens in late summer.

Height: 75 to 100 ft. Maple family

BLACK MAPLE is considered by some a species distinct from Sugar Maple. Others rank it simply as a variety with more shallow lobes and even fewer teeth. The bark is similar to that of Sugar Maple: dark gray, breaking into thin plates. Black Maple leaves are somewhat smaller than Sugar Maple, bright green above, yellowish and hairy beneath. The wood is reputed harder than Sugar Maple. Both Black and Sugar Maple are tapped in early spring when the sap flows. About 30 gallons of the watery, slightly sweet sap are boiled down to yield a gallon of golden brown syrup.

Height: 60 to 100 ft. Maple family

RED MAPLE lives up to its name in every season. In early spring, before the leaves appear, the blunt, red buds open, and clusters of red and orange flowers hang from the reddish twigs. As the leaves unfold, they too are reddish, gradually turning to green, paler underneath, with triangular lobes and small teeth. But the veins and the leafstalk keep their reddish tint all summer. The ripening fruit is red also. Red Maple is a widespread tree of swamps, river banks, and moist hill slopes. The soft, close-grained, light-brown wood is used for boxes, novelties, and woodenware.

Height: 60 to 80 ft. Maple family

SILVER MAPLE or Soft Maple has large, deeply lobed leaves that are pale green above and whitish below, with some hairs along the veins. One form has leaves deeply cut and indented. In fall they lack the brilliant colors of Red and Sugar Maples, turning dull yellow instead. The grayish bark is smooth, becoming furrowed and scaly with age. Silver Maple is a tree of river banks and bottomlands. It grows rapidly and is planted along streets for shade. It is also used as an ornamental. The white, soft wood is suited for millwork, spools, and small articles.

Height: 80 to 100 ft. Maple family

MOUNTAIN MAPLE, also called Dwarf Maple, is a small, shrubby tree of eastern mountains. Leaves, usually three-lobed, with small teeth, turn brilliant yellow and red in fall. The cluster of small greenish flowers with narrow petals forms an erect spike—unusual in Maples. Fruits, in hanging clusters, are red. The bark is smooth, thin, green when young, becoming reddish-brown with age. Another small Maple of eastern mountains is Striped Maple or Moosewood. Its smooth, greenish bark has thin, white stripes; the leaves are large, broad, and round-ed at the base.

Height: 15 to 20 ft. Maple family

Mountain Maple

BROADLEAF MAPLE has the largest leaf of any Maple. The leaf itself is 8 to 12 in. across and the petiole or leaf-stalk is 10 to 12 in. long. The thick leaf is five-lobed and deeply cut, dark green above and paler beneath. The Broadleaf Maple prefers bottomland soil, but grows in foothills and low mountains into Canada and Alaska where there is enough water. The bark is brownish and rough, with scaly ridges. The wood is light brown, similar to that of Sugar Maple. It is valued in the West, where hardwoods are relatively scarce, for veneer, furniture, and woodenware.

Height: 80 to 100 ft. Maple family

ROCKY MOUNTAIN MAPLE is also called Dwarf Maple and rightly so, for it is more typically a shrub than a tree. It should not be confused with Mountain Maple (p. 123), which is also called Dwarf Maple. The leaves are quite variable. Some look like a coarse Red Maple leaf; some have only three lobes and an almost straight base. Occasionally, leaves are cut so deeply that they appear to be compound. The veins are yellow and prominent. Rocky Mountain Maple is found where the soil is moist. It prefers higher altitudes in the southern part of its range.

Height: 10 to 20 ft. Maple family

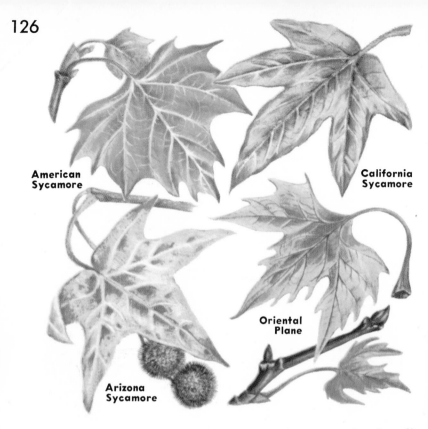

American Sycamore

California Sycamore

Oriental Plane

Arizona Sycamore

SYCAMORES or Plane Trees beautify stream banks all through the East and in some of the valleys of the Southwest. The three native species are characterized by bark which peels off in large brown sheets, revealing the cream-colored fresh bark beneath and giving the trunk an attractive mottled appearance. Of the native species, the American Sycamore is best known and most common. The leaves are almost heart-shaped, three- to five-lobed, thick, light green above, paler and hairy below. The base of the leafstalk is hollow, concealing the winter bud. Fruits are the typical "buttonballs." The hard, yellowish to brown, coarse-grained wood is used for furniture, boxes, and woodenware.

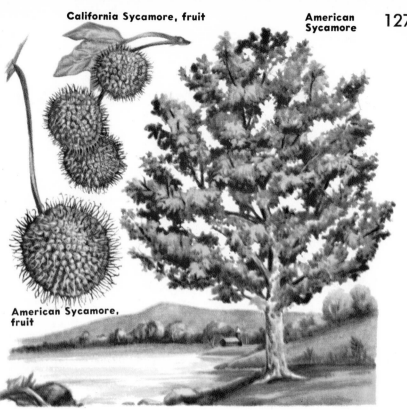

California Sycamore, fruit

American Sycamore

American Sycamore, fruit

The California and Arizona Sycamores are more limited in range. The California tree is very much like the eastern Sycamore but the fruits are not single, but in a string of three or four balls. The Arizona Sycamore is similar, with larger leaves and longer lobes. Along city streets and in parks, the Oriental and London Planes are often planted as ornamentals and for shade. These trees do well in the unfavorable environment of cities. The seeds of these Sycamores resemble those of our western species. The leaves of the London Plane are less lobed than our common Sycamore.

Height: 60 to 100 ft. Plane Tree family

California

Arizona

American

Cabbage Palmetto

PALMS AND PALMETTOS form a group quite separate from other trees. They are related more to Lilies, Bananas, Bamboo, and Grasses than to ordinary trees such as Oaks and Maples. Their leaves have parallel veins and the wood develops differently. In the tropics, this large and ancient group of plants is very important. The Royal Palm of Central America, most majestic of the Palms, occurs sparingly in Florida. Here also we find the Cabbage or Sabal Palmetto, with its cluster of large, fan-shaped leaves topping a thick base stalk, 20 to 30 ft. high. This reaches its largest size along the West Coast, where it is common near the beaches. Cabbage Palmetto is named for the large, edible bud or "cabbage" crowning the stem.

Our native western Palm, the Washington Palm, is very restricted in its natural range, but has been widely planted here and abroad. It is our largest native species. This is a Palm of the desert, and grows in canyons and near waterholes. The fan-shaped leaves, 4 to 5 ft. across, are usually split and frayed by the wind. The small white flowers develop into round black fruits which were used as food by desert Indians. The western Yucca or Joshua Tree is a member of the Lily family and is related to the Palms.

Height: 20 to 30 ft. (Cabbage Palmetto); 40 to 60 ft. (Washington Palm).
Palm family

Washington Palm

Cabbage Palmetto

Shagbark Hickory

Mockernut Hickory

HICKORIES and their relatives constitute an important group of nut-bearing trees. Some have been naturalized and cultivated to produce important crops. As wild trees of open forests, Hickories are at their best: large, well-shaped trees with straight trunks and heavy limbs. Hick-

Bitternut Hickory

Pecan

ories have alternate, compound, fragrant leaves. The first pair of leaflets, from the tip of the leaf, is usually largest. Hickory wood is prized as fuel for outdoor cooking and smoking meats. It is used for tool handles and articles which call for tough, light wood.

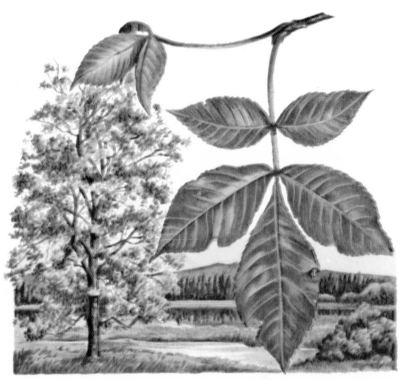

SHAGBARK HICKORY has gray bark with long, loose scales—even shaggier and looser than those of Sycamore. The leaves are alternate and compound, with five or seven rather broad, toothed leaflets. The stout twigs bear large brown buds. The nuts have thick husks, but the shell is thin and the meat is edible and sweet. These are the hickory nuts occasionally seen in stores. Shagbark Hickory prefers rich, moist soil and is often found with Oaks in open woods. In spring the opening of Hickory buds, with their greatly enlarged bud scales, is a sight worth seeing.

Height: 60 to 80 ft. Walnut family

MOCKERNUT is indeed a mockery: the nut has a thick husk and little or no meat inside the heavy, hard shell. The bark of this upland tree is gray, thick, and furrowed. The ridges between the furrows are typically rounded. The leaflets (seven or nine to a leaf) are narrower than those of Shagbark. The reddish-brown twigs and the paler buds are hairy—a point that helps in winter identification. Mockernut has large, oval buds with overlapping scales. The flower, as in other Hickories, is a greenish catkin. The tough, dark-brown, elastic wood is similar to that of Shagbark.

Height: 40 to 60 ft. Walnut family

BITTERNUT is sometimes called Swamp Hickory because of its preference for wet soils. The bark is grayish brown, scaly, with shallow furrows. Twigs are yellowish brown and dotted. The bright, sulfur-yellow buds of Bitternut are a sure means of identification. Note the seven to nine leaflets to each leaf—narrow, pointed, and finely toothed, bright green above, pale beneath. The nut is small, thin-shelled, and in a pointed husk. Perhaps because of its very bitter nut, people and animals leave more seeds of Bitternut to grow, giving the tree a better chance to survive. At any rate, the tree is common.

Height: 60 to 80 ft. Walnut family

PECAN is a native southern Hickory which has been transformed into an important, cultivated crop tree. It is also planted as an ornamental. The long, pointed nuts, developed in new thin-shelled varieties, are a staple luxury food. They grow in a thin, slightly winged husk. Pecan has a gray-brown, deeply furrowed bark. Twigs are somewhat hairy, the bud yellowish. The leaf is long and pendent, with 11 to 17 narrow, finely toothed, slightly curved leaflets. Pecan is a large tree—the largest of the Hickories. Its wood is more brittle and has less uses than other very similar species.

Height: 80 to 100 ft. Walnut family

Original range

BLACK WALNUT is a prized hardwood. The brown, fine-grained wood is used for gunstocks, furniture, and cabinets. Black Walnut is a tree of rich, open woods and roadsides and has often been used as a shade tree. The large, fragrant leaves have 15 or more leaflets, each finely toothed and ending in a long point. They are smooth above, hairy below. The round nut grows in a thick green husk, from which the pioneers made a brown dye. It has a dark, irregular, hard shell that is hard to crack, but the sweet, edible, very distinctly flavored kernel makes the effort worth while.

Height: 80 to 100 ft. Walnut family

BUTTERNUT or White Walnut is a spreading tree, smaller than Black Walnut, with light gray bark that breaks
into elongated flat ridges. It is a tree of stream banks,
roadsides, and open woods, preferring rich, well-drained
soil. The leaf, similar to that of Black Walnut, has fewer
(7 to 17) and slightly broader, more hairy leaflets. The
edible nut, in a greenish, gummy husk, is long and pointed.
Other species of Walnut are cultivated in the West.
The English or Persian Walnut (native
of the Middle East) is grown in
orchards to produce the thin-shelled
commercial Walnuts.

Height: 30 to 50 ft. Walnut family

BOXELDER is an exceptional Maple, the only one with compound leaves. Its leaves grow oppositely on thick green twigs, with three to five large, coarsely toothed leaflets. The grayish-brown bark is thin, cracking into interlacing fissures. The fruits, typical paired keys of Maple, grow in drooping clusters. Boxelder is widespread through the Central States along streams, roads, and fields. It grows rapidly and has been used as a shade tree in prairie towns, though it is not nearly so attractive as other Maples. It is also used in shelterbelt plantings.

Height: 40 to 60 ft. Maple family

AILANTHUS or Tree of Heaven is a native of China, brought to this country as food for silkworms. It has spread rapidly, growing mainly in moist locations. It thrives in city backyards and lots, and seems invincible against smoke, dirt, and insects. Ailanthus is a short-lived "weed" tree which may temporarily crowd out more desirable species. The long, compound, fern-like leaves have from 15 to 31 leaflets, each lance-shaped with smooth edges. At the base of each leaflet is a small tooth, with a swollen, scent gland. The ill-smelling male flowers and the small female flowers are borne on separate trees. The smooth, striped, gray-brown bark cracks with age.

Height: 50 to 80 ft. Quassia family

Smooth Sumac

Staghorn Sumac

SUMACS are a group of thick, pithy-twigged shrubs and small trees. Even the largest rarely grow more than 20 ft. high; most are smaller. They grow in open fields and road-sides, spreading rapidly in most well-drained soils to form thickets. Staghorn Sumac, the most common, is recognized by the hairy twigs and leaves, which are almost white beneath. Leaves turn red in the fall. Smooth Sumac is similar but, as its name indicates, lacks the hairy twigs. The leaves are generally like those of Staghorn Sumac, though leaflets may be almost entire or deeply cut on the margins.

Staghorn Sumac

Smooth Sumac

Dwarf Sumac   **Poison-sumac**

The Dwarf Sumac is not much smaller than other species. Its leaves are distinctly different, with edges entire and leaflets a bright, shiny green. The leafstalk between the leaflets is winged. Fruits, red when ripe, form fairly compact clusters. Poison-sumac is a swamp-loving, attractive species. Leaflets are shiny green, with entire edges turning brilliant orange and red in fall. Woe unto anyone who picks them! They are more poisonous to the touch than poison ivy. The yellowish-white berries in loose clusters aid in identification during winter.

Height: 10 to 30 ft. Cashew family

Dwarf Sumac (blue)

Poison-sumac (red)

Black Ash

White Ash

Red Ash

Black Ash

White Ash

Red Ash

ASHES are to baseball what Maples are to bowling. Bats and other sporting goods are made from their tough, fine-grained, elastic wood, which has other uses too. Of about 20 species of native Ash, most are eastern trees. All have opposite, compound leaves, catkin-like flowers, and winged seeds in drooping clusters.

WHITE ASH is the most common and best-known eastern Ash. It is a forest tree of rich, moist soils, often found with Oaks, Hickories, and Maples. White Ash grows tall, with a broad crown. The bark is gray, with interlacing fissures and ridges. Leaves and twigs are opposite. The compound leaves usually have seven oval leaflets, dark green above, paler and silvery beneath, each with a few irregular blunt teeth. They turn yellow or purplish in autumn. Fruits are single "keys" with a long narrow wing. They form in spring and hang in drooping clusters till they drop off in late fall.

Height: 60 to 90 ft. Olive family

BLACK ASH is a northern tree, common in swamps and in moist soils. Its dark green leaves look black in the forest shade. The bark is dark gray, with shallow, interlocking cracks. The twigs are smooth, gray, with light lenticels and dark buds. The 7 to 11 leaflets are finely toothed, hairy along the large veins, and without a stalk. The winged fruits of Black Ash have a conspicuous notch at the base. So do fruits of the angular-twigged Blue Ash of the Central States. The latter, however, are shorter and wider than Black Ash fruits. The wood of Black Ash is heavy, brown, and tough.

Height: 50 to 80 ft. Olive family

RED ASH is a small, spreading tree with typical Ash bark and branching. The leaf is like that of White Ash but is sometimes hairy along the leaf stem. The fruit is narrower than in other ashes. In the East a variety of it, known as Green Ash, is identified by smooth twigs and shoots. Typical Red Ash twigs are velvety. Farther west, these two forms—the Green and Red—seem to merge. Red Ash is sometimes planted as a shade or shelterbelt tree, especially west of the Mississippi. The wood, light brown in color and similar to White Ash, is used for tool handles, baskets, and sporting goods.

Height: 40 to 60 ft. Olive family

MOUNTAIN-ASH, in spite of its name, is not an Ash at all but is in the same family as Hawthorns and Apples. Several species, all northern and preferring rich mountain soil, have small white flowers in flattened clusters. The compound, Ash-like leaves grow alternately on the stem and have about 13 to 15 leaflets, evenly toothed. The bark is smooth, gray-brown, similar to Cherry. The showy red berries are a favorite winter food of song and game birds. A European species, Rowan Tree, with orange fruit, is widely cultivated in northern states as a lawn ornamental.

Height: 15 to 25 ft. Rose family

BLACK LOCUST is a tree valued as an ornamental for street planting and as a soil binder in stabilizing eroded land. It is a tall, somewhat slender, irregular tree with short branches. The smooth twigs are distinctive in having a pair of small thorns at the base of each leaf. Leaves are alternate and compound, with small, oval leaflets, 13 to 15 to a leaf. The leaflets have smooth edges and are silvery below. The flowers of Black Locust, creamy white and fragrant, unfold in long clusters before the leaves are well developed. The bark is a dark gray, rough, and broken into branching ridges. Black Locust is bothered by borers and fungus pests, but the wood, resistant to rotting, makes excellent fenceposts (Plate on p. 148.)

Height: 30 to 50 ft. Pea family

HONEY LOCUST, like Black Locust, is widely planted outside of its natural range. It is larger than Black Locust and thornier. Sometimes the entire trunk is encircled by long, branching thorns. The bark, nearly black, is smooth on young trees, breaking into long, scaly ridges. The leaves are similar to those of Black Locust but more narrow, and may be twice compounded with each leaflet like a compound leaf. The flowers are greenish and small. They hang in clusters 2 to 3 inches long from the base of the leaves. The flat, reddish-brown seed pods grow about a foot long and contain a sweet, sticky pulp in addition to the hard seeds. These pods are sometimes fed to cattle. The wood of Honey Locust is used for fenceposts, construction, and ties. (Plate on p. 149.)

Height: 60 to 100 ft. Pea family

148

BLACK LOCUST (text on p. 147)

HONEY LOCUST (text on p. 147)

KENTUCKY COFFEE-TREE is so named because pioneers in that state made a bitter drink from its seeds. This odd tree, which has only one relative—a Chinese species—has a wide range, but nowhere is it common. The dark trunk, with furrows and ridges, and the scaly, thick twigs identify the tree in winter and spring. Kentucky Coffee-tree does not leaf out till very late. Leaves are large, twice compounded, with oval, pointed, widely spaced leaflets. The fruit, a large heavy bean, is similar to but thicker than that of Honey Locust. The soft, brown, coarse wood is too scarce to be of use.

Height: 75 to 100 ft. Pea family

BUCKEYES are a small group of native trees with several relatives south of the Mexican border. They are unusual in several ways. Their fruits, though large and attractive, are inedible. (It is the white spot on the brown nut that gives the Buckeye its name.) The compound leaves grow opposite on thick twigs, but the leaflets, instead of spreading feather-like as they do in Ash or Ailanthus, radiate out like the fingers of your hand. These distinctive leaves identify Buckeyes and Horsechestnut. Eastern Buckeyes have yellow or pink flowers in loose clusters. The California species has a smooth, pear-shaped fruit and white flowers. Their nectar, poisonous to bees, creates a serious problem. (Plate on p. 152.)

Height: 20 to 40 ft. Horsechestnut family

HORSECHESTNUT has been carried from the Balkans north into Europe and thence westward to this country. It is planted along streets and in parks, and is an old favorite with its spreading, rounded shape and its massive clusters of flowers. The Horsechestnut twig is an ideal one to study in winter. The large, resinous buds on its sides and end are easily examined. Place a twig indoors in water and watch the buds slowly swell and burst. Note the scars left by last year's bud scales. See how much the tree has grown by tracing back from one group of bud-scale scars to another. Recognize Horsechestnut by its opposite, compound leaves, like those of Buckeye but coarser and with leaflets wider near the apex. The large nuts, which fall as the spiny husks open, are attractive to see but are bitter and inedible, as any boy who has been tempted by them can testify. (Plate on p. 153.)

Height: 50 to 80 ft. Horsechestnut family

152

BUCKEYE (text on p. 151)

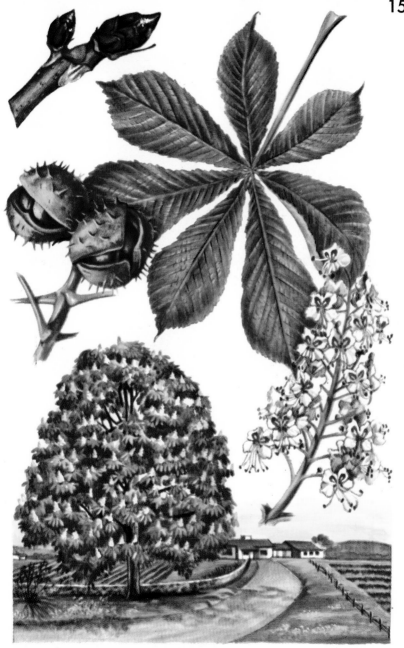

HORSECHESTNUT (text on p. 151)

NATIONAL FORESTS

National forests are recreation areas and excellent places to study trees and forestry. Our main national forest areas are shown in green on the map above. These are your recreational areas; use them for visits or longer vacations. Information about specific forests may be obtained from the following regional offices:

1 **Northern Region:** Federal Bldg., Missoula, Montana 59801

2 **Rocky Mountain Region:** Federal Center, Bldg. 85, Denver, Colorado 80225

3 **Southwestern Region:** 510 Second St., N.W., Albuquerque, New Mexico 87101

4 **Intermountain Region:** Forest Service Bldg., Ogden, Utah 84401

5 **California Region:** 630 Sansome St., San Francisco, California 94111

6 **Pacific Northwest Region:** Post Office Building, Portland, Oregon 97208

7 **Eastern Region:** 6816 Market St., Upper Darby, Pennsylvania 19082

8 **Southern Region:** 50 Seventh St., N.E., Atlanta, Georgia 30309

9 **North Central Region:** 623 North Second St., Milwaukee, Wisconsin 53203

BOOKS ON TREES listed below include a variety of informational guides and manuals. These and many others will help you toward a better understanding of trees and more skill in identifying them. Also available are many Federal and state publications on trees, forestry, and related subjects.

U.S. Department of Agriculture: TREES, THE YEARBOOK OF AGRICULTURE, 1949, U.S. Govt. Printing Office, Washington 25, D.C. A top reference volume on trees, forests, and forestry.

Petrides, George A.: A FIELD GUIDE TO TREES AND SHRUBS, Houghton Mifflin Co., Boston, 1958. Another useful guide in the Peterson series covering trees, shrubs and vines of northeastern and central North America.

Harlow, William M.: TREES OF EASTERN UNITED STATES AND CANADA, McGraw-Hill Book Co., New York, 1942. A handy, non-technical guide to the region indicated.

Harrar, E. S., and Harrar, J. G.: GUIDE TO SOUTHERN TREES, McGraw-Hill Book Co., New York, 1946. This is a handy, well-illustrated field guide to southern trees.

Eliot, W. A., and McLean, G. B.: FOREST TREES OF THE PACIFIC COAST, G. P. Putnam's Sons, New York, 1938. A complete guide to the principal western species.

U. S. Department of Agriculture: AGRICULTURE HANDBOOK #41, CHECK LIST OF NATIVE AND NATURALIZED TREES OF THE U.S., 1953, U.S. Govt. Printing Office, Washington 25, D.C. Principal source of scientific and common names.

MUSEUMS AND BOTANICAL GARDENS are good

places to study trees. Museums may have exhibits of leaves, twigs, wood, fruits, or systematic groupings of trees. Local museums, not listed below, may also contain interesting exhibits. Study labeled growing trees in parks, botanical gardens, or special tree collections (arboretums). Don't forget National Parks, Monuments, and Forests, and state parks and forests for protected stands of native species.

MUSEUMS

Albany, N. Y.: New York State Museum

Chicago: Chicago Natural History Museum

New York: American Museum of Natural History

Washington: U.S. National Museum

PARKS, BOTANICAL GARDENS, AND ARBORETUMS

Ann Arbor, Mich.: Nicholls Arboretum

Berkeley, Calif.: Univ. of Calif. Botanical Garden

Boston: Boston Public Gardens

Chicago: Brookfield Zoo

Chicago: Lincoln Park

Coconut Grove, Fla.: Fairchild Tropical Gardens

Illinois: Cook County Forest Preserves

Jamaica Plain, Mass.: Arnold Arboretum

Kennett Square, Pa.: Longwood Gardens

Lisle, Ill.: Morton Arboretum

Miami: U.S.D.A. Plant Station

Muncie, Ind.: Huntington Arboretum

New Haven, Conn.: Marsh Botanical Garden, Yale Univ.

New London, Conn.: Conn. College for Women Arboretum

Petersham, Mass.: Harvard Forest

St. Louis: St. Louis Botanical Garden

St. Paul, Minn.: Como Park

San Francisco: Golden Gate Park

Washington: St. Elizabeth's Hospital Grounds

Washington: U.S. National Arboretum

SCIENTIFIC NAMES

Following are the scientific names of species illustrated in this book. Heavy type indicates pages where illustrations occur. The genus name is first, then the species. If the genus name is abbreviated, it is the same as the genus name mentioned just before it.

20 Pinus strobus.
21 Pinus lambertiana.
22 Pinus rigida.
23 Pinus palustris.
24 Pinus ponderosa.
25 Pinus contorta.
26 Pinus virginiana.
27 Pinus edulis.
28 Picea engelmannii.
29 Black: Picea mariana.
   White: P. glauca.
   Red: P. rubens.
30 Tamarack: Larix laricina.
   Western: L. occidentalis.
31 Pseudotsuga menziesii.
32 Abies concolor.
33 Abies balsamea.
34 Giant: Sequoia gigantea.
   Redwood: S. sempervirens.
35 Tsuga canadensis.

36 Juniperus osteosperma.
37 Alligator: Juniperus deppeana.
   Sierra: J. occidentalis.
38 Juniperus virginiana.
39 Thuja occidentalis.
40 Taxodium distichum.
41 Nyssa sylvatica.
42 Diospyros virginiana.
44 Cornus florida.
45 Catalpa speciosa.
46 Cercis canadensis.
47 Maclura pomifera.
48 Umbrella: Magnolia tripetala.
   Sweetbay: M. virginiana.
49 Cucumber: Magnolia acuminata.
   Southern: M. grandiflora.
51 Magnolia soulangeana.
52 Arbutus menziesii.
53 Umbellularia californica.
54 Salix nigra.

55 Salix babylonica:
56 Crack: Salix fragilis.
   Peachleaf: S. amygdaloides.
   Sandbar: S. interior.
   Pussy: S. discolor.
57 Ulmus americana.
58 Winged: Ulmus alata.
   Slippery: U. rubra.
59 Rock: Ulmus thomasii.
   Cedar: U. crassifolia.
60 Celtis occidentalis.
61 Amelanchier canadensis.
62 Carpinus caroliniana.
63 Ostrya virginiana.
64 Ilex opaca.
65 Fagus grandifolia.
66 Choke: Prunus virginiana.
   Wild Black: P. serotina.
67 Pin: Prunus pensylvanica.
   Wild Plum: P. americana.
70 Paper: Betula papyrifera.
   Gray: B. populifolia.
   White: B. pendula.
71 Yellow: B. alleghaniensis.
   River: B. nigra.
   Sweet: B. lenta.
75 Red: Alnus rubra.
   Speckled: A. rugosa.
   White: A. rhombifolia.
76 Oxydendrum arboreum.
77 Cascara: Rhamnus purshiana.
   Carolina: R. caroliniana.
78 Populus tremuloides.
79 Populus grandidentata.
80 Populus deltoides.
81 Tilia americana.
82 Chestnut: Castanea dentata.
83 Tanbark-oak:
   Lithocarpus densiflorus
86 Quercus alba.
87 Quercus stellata.
88 Quercus macrocarpa.
89 Quercus lyrata.
90 Quercus prinus.
91 Quercus muehlenbergii.
92 Quercus bicolor.
93 Quercus virginiana.
94 Quercus gambelii.
95 Quercus agrifolia.
98 Quercus velutina.
99 Quercus rubra.
100 Quercus falcata.
101 Quercus palustris.

102 Quercus coccinea.
103 Quercus marilandica.
104 Quercus nigra.
105 Quercus imbricaria.
106 Quercus phellos.
107 Quercus chrysolepis.
108 Sassafras albidum.
109 Liriodendron tulipfera.
111 Ashe: Crataegus ashei.
   English: C. oxyacantha.
   Little Hip: C. spathulata.
   Cockspur: C. crus-galli.
112 Crataegus pedicellata.
113 Liquidambar styraciflua.
114 White: Morus alba.
   Red: M. rubra.
118 Acer platanoides.
119 Acer saccharum.
120 Acer nigrum.
121 Acer rubrum.
122 Acer saccharinum.
123 Acer spicatum.
124 Acer macrophyllum.
125 Acer glabrum.
126 American: Platanus
   occidentalis.
   California: P. racemosa.
   Arizona: P. wrightii.
   Oriental: P. orientalis.
128 Sabal palmetto.
129 Washingtonia filifera.
132 Carya ovata.
133 Carya tomentosa.
134 Carya cordiformis.
135 Carya illinoensis.
136 Juglans nigra.
137 Juglans cinerea.
138 Acer negundo.
139 Ailanthus altissima.
140 Staghorn: Rhus typhina.
   Smooth: R. glabra.
141 Dwarf: Rhus copallina.
   Poison: Toxicodendron vernix.
143 Fraxinus americana.
144 Fraxinus nigra.
145 Fraxinus pennsylvanica.
146 Sorbus americana.
148 Robinia pseudoacacia.
149 Gleditsia triacanthos.
150 Gymnocladus dioica.
152 Aesculus glabra.
153 Aesculus hippocastanum.

INDEX

An asterisk (*) denotes pages that illustrate the tree or its parts. **Bold type** designates pages containing more extensive information.

Acorns, 82-83, *85, *97
Ailanthus, *139
Alders, *75
Alligator Juniper, *37
American Aspen, *78
American Basswood, *81
American Beech, *65
American Elm, *57
American Holly, *64
American Hornbeam, *62
American Sycamore, *126-*127
Annual rings, *13
Arboretums, 156
Arizona Sycamore, *126, 127
Ashe Hawthorn, *111
Ashes:
 Black, *142, **144**
 Blue, 144
 Green, 145
 Mountain-, *146
 Red, *142, **145**
 White, *142, **143**
Aspens, *78-*79

Baldcypress, *40
Balsam Fir, 32-*33
Bark, *10 12-13
Basket Oak, 92
Basswood, *81
Bay, *53
Beeches, *65
 Blue, *62
Bigcone Spruce, 31
Bigtooth Aspen, *79
Birches:
 Black, *71, **74**
 Canoe, *70, **72**
 Cherry, *71, **74**
 Gray, *70, **72**
 Paper, *70, **72**
 Red, *71, **73**
 River, *71, **73**
 Sweet, *71, **74**
 White, *70, *72, **74**
 Yellow, *71, **73**

Bitternut, *131, **134**
Black Ash, *142, **144**
Black Birch, *71, **74**
Blackgum, *41
Blackjack Oak, *96, *97, **103**
Black Locust, 147, *148
Black Maple, *120
Black Oak, *96-**98**
Black Spruce, 28, *29
Black Walnut, *136
Black Willow, *54
Botanical gardens, 156
Boxelder, 117, *138
Broadleaf Maple, *124
Broadleaf trees, 3, *9, 41-153
Buckeyes, 151, *152
Buckthorns, *77
Buds, *11
Bunchberry, 43
Bur Oak, *84, *85, **88**
Butternut, *137

Cabbage Palmetto, *128, 129
California-laurel, *53
California Live Oak, *84, *85, **95**
California Red Fir, 33
California Sycamore, *126-*127
California White Oak, 94
Canadian Spruce, 28
Canoe Birch, *70, **72**
Canyon Live Oak, *96, *97, **107**
Carolina Buckthorn, *77
Cascara Buckthorn, *77
Catalpa, 43, *45
Cedar Elm, *59
Cedars, *38-*39
Cherries: Bird, 69
 Choke, *66, **68**
 Pin, *67, **69**
 Red, **69**
 Wild, *66-*69
Cherry Birch, *71, **74**
Chestnut, *82, 90

Chestnut Oak, *84, *85, **90**
Chinkapin Oak, *84, *85, **91**
Choke Cherry, *66, **68**
Christmas trees, 33
Coast Live Oak, *84, *85, **95**
Cockspur Haw, *111
Coffee-tree, Kentucky, *150
Conifers, 3, *9, 18-40
Conservation, 14, 16
Cottonwoods, *80
Crack Willow, *56
Cucumber Magnolia, *49, 50
Cypress, Bald-, *40

Desert Juniper, 36-37
Dogwoods, 43-*44
Douglas-fir, *31, 33
Dwarf Sumac, *141

Eastern Buckeye, 151
Eastern Red-cedar, *38
Eastern White Pine, *19, **20**
Elms: American, *57
 Cedar, *59
 Rock, *59
 Slippery, *58
 Winged, *58
Engelmann Spruce, *28, 29
English Hawthorn, *111
English Walnut, 137

Firs, *32-*33
 Douglas-, *31, 33
Flowering Cherry, 67
Flowering Dogwood, 43, *44
Flowers, *10-*11
Forests, U.S., 154
Fruits, *10-*11

Gambel Oak, *84, *85, **94**
Giant Sequoia, *34
Gray Birch, *70, **72**
Green Stick, 108